DELIA AND NEMESIS
THE ELEGIES OF
ALBIUS TIBULLUS

*Introduction, Translation and
Literary Commentary*

George W. Shea

University Press of America,® Inc.
Lanham • New York • Oxford

Copyright © 1998
University Press of America,® Inc.
4720 Boston Way
Lanham, Maryland 20706

12 Hid's Copse Rd.
Cumnor Hill, Oxford OX2 9JJ

Library of Congress Cataloging-in-Publication Data

Tibullus.
(Elegiae. English)
Delia and Nemesis : the elegies of Albius Tibullus / introduction,
translation, and literary commentary, George W. Shea.
p.   cm.
Includes bibliographical references.
l. Elegiac poetry, Latin—Translations into English. 2. Rome—
Poetry. I. Shea, George W. II. Title.
PA6788.E5S54 1998   874'.01—dc21   98-35696 CIP

ISBN 0-7618-1226-1 (pbk: alk. ppr.)

This book is dedicated to my daughter Susan,
fellow classicist, who encouraged me in this work

Contents

Preface

This book was written primarily for readers who cannot read Latin but who wish to become acquainted with and enjoy Latin poetry. If one is to serve such readers, one must address three requirements. First, the inaccessible Latin text must be made available to them in a translation that is both accurate and appealing, that is couched in a diction which is clear, natural and, hopefully, not without grace. Second, such readers must also be provided with some understanding of the historical, cultural and mythological data needed to understand the text. These data, especially those which are based on myth, function in the Latin poetic text as a secondary signifying system, without knowledge of which interpretation of the text becomes nearly impossible. Finally, since many of these readers may have had little exposure to classical rhetoric and the critical tradition of antiquity, they must also be provided with some guidance as they undertake a critical reading of a Latin text in translation. It is my intention in this book to supply these three needs in a format which is inviting and easy to use, at the same time provoking students to undertake their own imaginative but disciplined engagement of the poetic texts before them. At the conclusion of this general introduction, therefore, the reader will find that each of Tibullus' sixteen elegies will be considered individually. An introduction containing the needed background knowledge, historical and mythic, will be given. This will be followed by a translation of the Latin text. To these a brief literary commentary, intended both to furnish critical background and to provoke critical reflection, will be added.

Why choose Tibullus for experimenting with this approach? For a number of reasons. First, as the discussion of his life will show, he is the quintessential Roman poet and a very good one as well. From the standpoint of practicality, the size of his collection, just sixteen poems of moderate length, make Tibullus an obvious choice. Beyond that, his poems have received a great deal of scholarly attention, albeit of uneven quality particularly in the nineteenth and early part of the twentieth century. Finally, the fact that relatively little is known of his life discourages the largely misguided impulse to read lyric poetry as a kind of autobiography. In the final analysis, of course, the preference of this translator and his obvious delight in Tibullus' work are also a major factor in his selection.

What do we know of Tibullus' life? Not a great deal. He was probably born sometime between 60 and 50 B.C. on a family estate in the Alban hills not far from Rome. He belonged to the Roman upper class and had as his patron the well known Marcus Valerius Messalla Corvinus, who, although he fought with Brutus and Cassius, the republican conspirators and assassins of Julius Caesar, later gave somewhat cautious support to the regime of Caesar's grandnephew, Augustus, for whom he also fought. Tibullus seems to have served with his patron in Aquitania in the west but was prevented by illness from accompanying him on his journey to the east. References to him in both Horace and Ovid suggest that Tibullus was a well-known writer of elegy in his own day and a brief medieval life tells us that he was handsome and refined in his taste in clothing. An epitaph, likewise late in origin, tells us that he died young and journeyed to the world of the dead as a companion to Vergil. Since we know that Vergil died in 19 B.C., it would seem that Tibullus died in either that year or early in the next year, probably while still in his thirties.

Tibullus was held in very high esteem as a poet in his own lifetime and in the age immediately after it. His fellow poet Ovid, refers to him as *cultus* or refined and the great literary critic, Quintilian, writing in the following century, applies to him the adjectives *tersus*, polished, and *elegans*, elegant, and ranks him first among the Roman elegists, a judgement which has troubled many modern critics, but which is, in my view, very likely to be correct. Tibullus' elegies come down to us in manuscripts which date from the fourteenth and fifteenth centuries and which contain the work of other poets as well, among them Lygdamus and Sulpicia, the only Latin poetess of his age whose work survives. The entire collection is referred to as the *Corpus Tibullianum*, the first two books of which contain our poet's elegies. For further discussion of the poet's life, his reputation in antiquity and the transmission of his works to the modern world, readers may usefully consult the works of Murgatroyd, Cairns and Putnam, which are cited in the bibliography at the end of this book.

In the last century and a half Tibullus' elegies have been carefully studied by classical scholars. Early efforts, however, produced very uneven results. Critics with seemingly little appreciation of the nature of poetic discourse and even less appreciation of Tibullus' unusual poetic sensibility, attempted to apply to his texts the rules of classical rhetoric and logic with disastrous results. When the elegies failed to measure up to the logical or sometimes mathematical forms that these paradigms called for, critics often went so far as to rearrange the lines of Tibullus' text in order to make it conform to their own prosaic and contrived expectations. More recent criticism has extricated itself from this morass of rhetorical misapprehensions. Studies like those of Cairns and Murgatroyd, editions like that of Putnam, upon which this translation is, with a few exceptions, based, and the translation and notes of Guy Lee are splendid additions to Tibullan scholarship, providing as they do a wealth of insights into linguistic, literary and cultural questions that are posed by the text. Even these critics, however, exhibit the traditional caution that characterizes classical scholarship. Their work focuses on the essential issues of language and textual emendation, on cultural and historical issues and especially upon genre and literary influence. This is, of course, well and good, but there remain places in the text where even these critics are satisfied to remark only that this or that is strange or disappointing or somehow difficult to understand. It is here, it seems to me, that students approaching Tibullus must bring new imaginative insights to their reading, being careful always to respect the results of the critical work already accomplished.

There can be no question, for example, that Cairn's insistence on viewing Tibullus as a Hellenistic poet, is correct and constitutes the proper starting point for any new reading of the poet. Tibullus belonged to a poetic tradition that is generally viewed as having started in the late fourth century in Greece and which was adopted by earlier Roman poets, often referred to as the Neoterics. This tradition and the poetry it produced bear the name Hellenistic and are marked by easily recognizable predilections and techniques, some of which have their roots in even earlier Greek lyric and epic poetry. For one thing these poets eschewed the writing of long heroic poems and attempted instead to understand the human condition by examining the seemingly insignificant or even trivial in life. Such an examination is accomplished by them not in a long narrative text but in a finely wrought, highly polished lyric of relatively few lines. In producing these poetic cameos, both learning and technique were of prime importance. The use of historical, legendary and mythic knowledge constitutes in the work of these poets a secondary system of signification, as we noted above, and these recondite allusions with their subtle implications make reading an extremely arduous business for a student unschooled in these matters. Of equal importance is the workmanship, the polish of these poems. Beneath a seemingly effortless poetic performance lies the results of painstaking work on language and metrics, on the arrangement of imagery and allusions and on the working out of the relationship of the poet to his reader. Generally, therefore, the message encoded in such a text is both indirect and subtle. The decoding calls for an equally painstaking effort on the part of the reader who must match the imaginative achievement of the poet with an imaginative endeavor of his own.

At the very heart of this Hellenistic poetic tradition lies, it seems to me, the belief that the world which we call real, is highly unstable and mutable, that things are not what they seem, or perhaps better, that things change and may be seen in different ways depending upon the perspective of the viewer. In the earliest Greek poetry of the Hellenistic age, therefore, we find a delight in taking what has been viewed as heroic or even divine and viewing it in a perfectly pedestrian and ordinary light. This striking change in focus was a technique that had its origins in the text of Homer, in which heroes and divinities are from time to time "humanized" and also in the texts of the archaic poets and fifth century dramatists like Euripides and Aristophanes. For the Hellenistic poets and their Roman descendants the fascination with this presentation of double or even multiple visions of things grew more and more important and became an essential tool for inscribing in their poems the fundamental instability of the phenomenal and noumenal worlds. It is not surprising, in the light of this, that elegy became a major form in this tradition. If the world is unreliable, if ideal visions necessarily shift and pass away, then we live in a world of disappointment, and disappointment breeds lament, the very life breath of elegy.

The techniques which the Hellenistic poet employed to encode this message of instability and disappointment are extremely subtle and constitute, it seems to me, the main reason why Tibullus has given his later critics such trouble. One must, for instance, take great care in understanding the lyric or elegiac voice in his poems. One must not, first of all, give way to the autobiographical fallacy, attributing to the figures in the text a historical reality which they are not meant to have. Obviously, like all writers, Tibullus drew upon people and things which he knew, people like Messalla, his patron, for example, in order to weave his poetic text. These figures, once in the text, however, are merely textual *personae*, as is the voice of the poet as it speaks in the elegy. This is, it seems to me, very important, and for this reason I shall distinguish carefully between Tibullus and the poet in the comments which follow my translations. By Tibullus I mean the conscious artist who created the text; by the poet I mean the figure in the text that constitutes the lyric or elegiac voice. Moreover, Tibullus' manipulation of that voice, the reader must be aware, is extremely subtle and clever. First, the reader will discover that the voice is almost always de-centered emotionally and psychologically. I do not mean, as at least one earlier critic has suggested, that the poet suffers from a serious mental disorder, psychosis or neurosis. I do mean that some circumstance, drinking, fear, illness, boredom or, in many cases, passion and despair, have altered his consciousness with the result that he does not think logically in the text. The train of his thought is governed instead by the seemingly unconscious association of ideas, itself driven by his own emotionally disordered state. Behind this apparent randomness, however, the hand of Tibullus himself, can of course be seen, if we make the effort. It is he, in the end, who actually structures the seemingly rambling discourse of the poet to achieve the effect he desires.

The ordering of elements in the text will generally be achieved not by employing the paradigms of classical logic and rhetorical theory but rather by the juxtaposition of syntactical markers and, above all, upon the disposition of imagery. Tibullus' elegies must, in fact be read with an eye to the changes in tenses and moods of verbs and to the choice and arrangement of images. The bolder the leap in thought, the bolder the image, the more seriously it must be taken. The new reader of Tibullus will do well, therefore, to ask frequently, "Why did he do that? Why did he choose that image?"

If Tibullus' use of the altered consciousness and de-centered voice made it easier for him to give his elegiac world greater verisimilitude, it also provided him with an opportunity for exploiting his text in another way, a strikingly modern way. The voice of the poet in these elegies is not just de-centered, it is also playful and unreliable. In short, the poet plays with the reader by withholding information, deliberately exciting expectations that are never fulfilled, even by lying to or deceiving him. The text becomes, therefore, a playing field, in which the poet and reader engage in a game of interpretative hide and seek. The elegiac voice of the poet cannot always be trusted and so the reader, by his own act of the imagination, must unmask him and hopefully decipher Tibullus' message as well.

What is it then that Tibullus was aiming at in the production of these polished poetic texts and what has he achieved? His genius lies, it seems to me, in his ability to draw his readers into a strange lyric and elegiac world that is unstable and therefore able to be perceived in different ways, and then to elicit from them an emotional and intellectual response which is multi-polar, that plays humor and grief, ecstasy and despair, the beautiful and the monstrous against one another in order to produce an elegiac catharsis. This catharsis is produced by the readers' response to the profound irony that characterizes Tibullus' bittersweet vision and by frequently contradictory but simultaneous emotions. It is necessary, therefore, in following his poetic rhythms to listen always for the striking of minor keys, even in the lightest of passages, and to be willing again and again to read the text against the grain. If this is done, the reader will, I think, experience and understand the catharsis Tibullus intended. It is, in fact, the achievement of such an emotional catharsis, the mingling of aesthetic pleasure with complex and distanced emotion, that characterizes all powerful poetry and which make Tibullus an even greater poet than he has generally been considered to be.

A final word on the translation of the elegies that follows. Tibullus wrote the elegies in a classical form known as the elegiac couplet. This couplet is composed of one dactylic hexameter line, followed by what is called the pentameter line, but which is in fact two half hexameter lines, divided in the center by a diaeresis. This pattern is repeated without alteration, but with frequent substitution of spondees for dactyls, from the beginning to the end of the poem. Both the inflected nature of the Latin language and this poetic form foster great artistry in the positioning of words and in the creation of an extremely tight and graceful diction. As a largely uninflected language, English lacks this capability. Nor can the metrical form of the elegiac couplet be transferred to English with any grace and naturalness. I have therefore not attempted to replicate Tibullus' metrical patterns, his artful arrangement of words or, in most case, his economy of expression and style. Some may argue with this and find my translations rather loose. So be it. What can be replicated, it seems to me, is Tibullus' clarity and the apparent simplicity of his diction. This I have strived to attain in a colloquial style couched in a loose iambic rhythm, whose lines vary in length from two to six feet. As I noted above, my primary concern was to find a vehicle which would be neither mannered nor forced, but which would appeal to the lyric sensibilities of contemporary readers. After all, if we do not reach them, we have accomplished little.

✦   ✦   ✦

N.B.: Readers should note that a set of asterisks in the text of the translation indicates missing words or lines in the Latin original.

Delia and Nemesis
The Elegies of Albius Tibullus

1.1

Introduction

Someone, perhaps his patron Messalla, perhaps his mistress Delia, has been chiding the poet about both his modest style of life and his unwillingness to rebuild his family's reduced fortune by participating in lucrative military expeditions. Perhaps he himself has been having misgivings on this count. In any case, he presents in this poem a justification of his own values and the kind of life they foster. The elegy is built around a contrast between the life of the military and commercial adventurer, who defies the violent forces of nature in order to acquire unnatural wealth, and the life of the farmer, who stands in awe of nature and cooperates with it both in his agricultural and pastoral activities and in his love for his mistress. The farmer's pleasures are simple: carefree rest and relaxation, the joys of love, enough to eat and drink and, in the end, a peaceful death with those he loves around him. Warriors like the great Messalla must risk injury and death in battle and on the sea, but even under the blistering Italian sun, in the summer when the Dog star rises, the poet lies carefree beneath a tree beside the cool waters of a stream. While Messalla brings back trophies with which to decorate his home, the poet carries out old rituals, honoring the traditional divinities: Ceres, the goddess of corn, Priapus, the fertility spirit whose statue often stood in a Roman garden, the Lares, the gods of home and hearth, and Pales, the protector of the herds.

1

Although this poem may be read as an interior monologue, the poet also imagines it as read or heard by both Messalla and by his mistress Delia, both of whom he addresses in it.   It can function, therefore, both as a polite refusal of Messalla's invitation to join him in a military campaign and as a plea to Delia to join the poet in the simple joys of country life, while they are both young enough to enjoy the delights of making love. In this way, the catalogue of his farms's attractions serves as an explanation to Messalla and an enticement to Delia, just as the death-bed scene envisioned is intended both as a contrast to Messalla's life, in which violent death is risked in campaigns overseas, and also as an argument for Delia's enjoying love while she may.

The poem is about the choice of a life style which fosters a life of moderation. It concludes with a clear declaration of the poet's choice: "This is the field I'm captain on, good soldier I," and also with the reaffirmation of the poet's belief that moderation is the best course in life, which is fraught with danger and surrounded by darkness and death. If this is the nature of life, neither great wealth nor crushing poverty is desirable. One needs to have a "little store." One needs to be able to despise both money and hunger.

Translation

Money's for some other man;
Let him pile up flame-yellow gold.
Let him own land,
Two-hundred acres tillable.
Let hard work dog him all day long,   5
Come terror when the foe draws near.
No sleep for him; the raucous horns
Of battle chase it far away.

But as for me, my little store of goods
May make me slave to idleness   10
As long as hearth burns bright
And fire's at my feet the whole night through.
I see myself a rustic, planting
In their seasons bending vines,
Planting tall young apple trees;   15
Green-thumbed, as long as Hope stands by

To offer heaps of fruit and brim
My basins with a sweet new wine.

I say my prayers. I say them when I see
They've hung a flowered necklace   20
Upon a lonely stump out in the fields,
Or on some old stone god who stands
Where roadways meet. Whatever fruit
The new year gives I set as gift
Before the farmer god. I pray   25
That there are always sheaves of wheat for you,
Golden Ceres, as a crown, plucked
From my fields and hung upon your temple door.
And I would set an old Priapus up,
A red-stained guard amid my trees,   30
And he would frighten birds away,
Shaking his blood-thirsty hook.
You Lares, home gods, receive your gifts as well.
You were the watchers of our fields
That once were rich and now are poor.   35
Those days a heifer fell to cleanse
A hundred cows, but now a tiny lamb
Is all the sacrifice our farm can make.
But still for you a lamb *will* fall,
And all around the village boys   40
Will cry "Io" and shout besides:
"Good harvest give us, good wine too!"

Now, now at last I could be satisfied
To live on but a little and...
Not give myself to journeys overseas;   45
But in the shade of one broad tree
Escape the torrid rising of the Dog,
Upon a bank where some small stream
Runs by. And no disgrace in picking up
A hoe from time to time, in prodding   50
Sluggish cows with a sharpened stick.
Nor loath to bring back in my arms
A lamb or baby goat

Handwritten margin notes (top, diagonal): *could he be talking to warriors? spare him + farmers. was war elsewhere*

Handwritten margin note (middle): *giving men away + to the gods.*

Handwritten margin note (bottom): *but he is*

That some forgetful mother left behind.

You thieves and wolves, please spare my little flock   55
And hunt your prizes in some vaster herd.
On this, my farm, year after year
My custom holds: to purify
The shepherd, sprinkle Pales, ghost of Peace,
With milk. Come to us, you divinities,   60
And don't be proud, too proud to take
The gifts our meager table gives,
Set out in simple earthenware
That's clean and pure; for farmers
Long ago first made these earthen jars   65
Molding them of soft and moistened clay.

What need have I of the money that my father had.
Of income which his father got
From barns of grain in years gone by?
A little crop's enough. Enough for me   70
If I may lie in bed, refresh
My body on a quilt that's mine.
And what a pleasure, lying there,
To hear the winds, relentless on and on,
To hold my woman in a soft embrace   75
And then at last to drift, carefree, to sleep,
Beside a fire that gives us joy
While winter wind unleashes freezing rain.

That's all I want. Let him be rich -
It's only right - the man who can endure   80
The angry sea, the dismal rain.
I cannot tell you how much gold,
How many emeralds I would throw away
Before I'd see some girl in tears
Because I'd gone abroad. It's right,   85
For you, for you, Messalla: all
Your marching off to war and all
Those battles on the sea, to deck
Your house with trophies that a foeman lost.

And me? The chains a lovely girl has forged   90
Now hold me tight, and I,
A watcher, sit before unopened doors.
Delia, my love, it's not men's praise
I want. As long as I'm with you,
They're free to call me lazy,   95
Idle, if they wish. It's you
I want to see in my last hour,
To touch with quivering fingers as I die.
O you will weep, my Delia,
When they place me on the bed of flame,   100
And you will kiss my cheek and sadly cry.
Yes, you will weep. Not iron
Is the forecourt of your heart,
No flint inside that tender heart itself.
And from that funeral, not a single girl   105
Or boy will come, dry-eyed, back home.
But, Delia, please don't offend my ghost with grief:
No streaming hair, no clawing of your tender cheeks.

Between this day and that, while fate allows,
Let's twine ourselves in love.   110
Soon death will come, head cowled in dark;
Soon sluggish age creeps in on us,
And it will be indecent then,
With hair turned white, to love
And whisper catch-words that were born of love.   115
It's now we have to clutch
At insubstantial, fleeting love,
While breaking down a door is free of shame
And getting up a fight is still a joy.

excluded lover. begging to be led in.

This is the field I'm captain on,   120
Good soldier I. You flags, you horns
Away from here! Give wounds to greedy men.
Give wealth as well. For me no worries now.
My little store is neatly piled
And I can say to hell with wealth,   125
To hell with hunger too.

Commentary

As we have seen, Tibullus builds this poem on a contrast between the life of a rich and powerful man and the life of a farmer, between the life of extravagance and the life of moderation. He argues in it that the latter is far preferable to him, given the essentially sad and gloomy nature of human existence, threatened as it is with the approach of old age and death.

The elegy's first structural principle lies in this contrast drawn between the poet himself, seen as an example of moderation and the "other man," seen as an example of extravagance. It begins with a direct statement of the situation of the "other man," who possesses gold and land but fear and anxiety as well. This statement is followed by a lengthy description of the poet's own rustic and pious life, both as it is in fact and as it is imagined by him. At the conclusion of this part of the poem the "other man" once again appears, first in the form of the poet's wealthier father and grandfathers and, further on, as anyone who is able to face the terrors of the stormy sea for the sake of profit. Nor is this second example of the "other man" left vague, for the poet soon reveals that he is in fact thinking of Messalla, his patron, a man who has successfully and properly , given his stature and his duties, risked the dangers of war for both glory and gain.

Messalla is not, however, the only "other" mentioned in the poem. In the following lines he protests to his mistress Delia that as long as he can be with her he cares not at all for those "others" who withhold praise from him because he refuses to follow his patron's example. After this indirect reference to the life of the "other man" the poet concludes with yet another direct but once again vague reference to the "greedy man" in the elegy's final statement of its basic contrast. What we find, then, is that this elegy, which presents a statement of the poet's own values, is punctuated by a series of references to the opposite values and the style of life they foster. These references are varied by the poet: now direct, now indirect, now present, now past, now vague, now specific.

The poem's second principle of organization is common to much of Tibullus' poetry and reflects his interest in the relationship of past to present and of both of these to both the real and ideal future. This elegy may be viewed in fact as a study of the relationship of the poet's past to his present condition and to both the inevitable and the longed for future.

This structural device is reflected in the juxtaposition of various verb forms. One can follow the poet's leaps of imagination and thought by tracing the patterns of present and past tense forms as well as the future, subjunctive and imperative forms that reflect his attitudes toward the life and death that are to come.

The poet's imagination transcends present reality and moves from it to the past and his family's former prosperity. It then leaps to the inevitable future, which will bring old age and death, and to the more proximate future he desires: the quiet country life and the love of his mistress. These shifts in mood and tense apply not only to the poet's own situation in life, but to the situation of the "other man" as well, something which gives the poem an especially rich, almost surreal temporal and modal texture.

As we examine the text more closely, we find that the poem begins in the realm of wish and longing as it relates to both self and other. Before long, however, it shifts to the poet's piety as a present reality and then, with that as a starting point, to a dream of idyllic rituals in the future. These in turn recall the rituals of the past, providing as we have noted, an historical reference to the "other man" in the form of the poet's wealthy ancestors. This reference to ancestors is, however, a fleeting one and its imagery is at once contrasted with the imagery of present ceremonies and, beyond that, with those which the poet expects to conduct in the future. And so the poet slips back into the realm of fantasy and desire, picturing himself in the shade of one of his trees or caring for his flocks. Concern for the animals brings him back to present, however, to his ritual observances once again, to commands to thieves and wolves to spare his flocks and to invitations to the gods to join his festivities. These temporal frames continue to shift with remarkable rapidity. The distant past of primitive farmers is recalled and, once again, the past life of his own family, only to give way once again to the poet's present state of mind, which drifts inevitably into the realm of imagination and longing for an idealized future.

After the poet's reference to Messalla, the living embodiment of the "other man," we return to his present condition as he conjures up visions of his own future death and funeral, visions which contain a mixture of the inevitable and the longed for future. This blending of the real and ideal future continues in the next lines as well, as the poet contrasts his present wish for his mistress' love with images of both age and death on the one hand and of youthful abandon and recklessness on the other. The poem concludes with a clear restatement of the poet's views and intentions and with the wishes and commands which follow logically from these.

 Tibullus' imagery provides yet a third principle of organization. Dominant images of objects, events, sounds and colors recur in the poem, sometimes to bind its parts together, sometimes to contrast the conditions or perspectives of the poet and the "other man," or even to suggest the fundamental instability of nature and of human existence. Thus the wealth of the "other man" is golden but so too is Ceres, the goddess of corn. The sound of horns is heard at the poem's beginning and again as it draws to a close. Land is a source of anxiety for the "other man," but a source of joy for the poet. Messalla hangs up trophies won in battle in his house, but the poet hangs sheaves of wheat in the temple of Ceres. Water is a danger for the "other man," but provides the poet with contentment. It can, however, threaten him as well in the form of a storm, a fact which demonstrates the fickleness of nature and hence the superiority of the poet's sensible responses to it. Water appears as well in the form of tears shed both by the "other man" as he departs for battle and for the poet at his funeral. Perhaps the most striking inversion of imagery is that of bed and fire, the source of comfort in one scene but of grief in another. This last contrast is further emphasized by the images of the two embraces given at two different moments: the embrace of the living and the embrace of the dead.

It is imagery as well that provides the key to understanding the elegy's apparently abrupt transitions. The poet attempts to give the impression that one bold image gives rise in his mind to a new turn of thought or fantasy. What seems at first a somewhat abrupt or even illogical change is rendered more natural by the resonances in the poem's imagery. For example, the shift from pastoral to amatory delights is slowly prepared for by gradual shifts in imagery. A woman appears fleetingly at first in the bedroom scene in the storm, then again briefly weeping for an absent lover. Hence Delia's subsequent appearance on center stage is not entirely surprising. Such intertwining of imagery is not always obvious at first reading. The shouts of the village boys at the festival described early in the poem become the youthful cries of anguish at the poet's imagined funeral, and these in turn become the sounds of youthful boisterousness at the poem's conclusion. Flowing hair at the funeral finds its echo in the white hair that makes an aged lover appear ridiculous. The images of storing and piling up at the beginning of the elegy and again at the end form a ring that binds the text together. And finally, the images of war and of military command which occur twice early in the poem contrast with the violence of the lovers and with the poet's final boast that he is a soldier in the combat of love. All of these images are important structural elements in the elegy, which relies upon their association for its graceful movement and bold transitions.

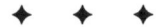

1.2

Introduction

The poet is at a party, perhaps at a tavern, and has had too much to drink. This elegy may be read, therefore, as if it were being spoken over a cup of wine, for it is cast in the form of an intoxicated man's rambling tale of woe told to a fellow drinker. Nor is the poet intoxicated with drink alone; he is drunk on both wine and love, and the influence of both join to muddle his wits as he keeps trying to sort out his situation and take charge of it. Unlike the preceding poem, which presented a fairly rational and coherent set of arguments for the poet's life style, this poem presents a struggle between the rational and irrational as they exist in the mind of a man contending with the effects of passion and drink.

As the elegy begins the poet seems resigned to having his wits drowned in wine. As he drifts toward sleep, however, his other intoxication, his love for Delia, captures his attention and he angrily recalls how his mistress has been locked up by her husband, or perhaps wealthy lover, and placed under guard. This challenge must be met, and so, painfully and slowly he begins to visualize a solution: Delia slipping out of bed, deceiving her guards and then opening her door to him. But his befuddled mind cannot sustain the effort required to trace her actions in detail, and so the poet slips into a digression about the deception of husbands and rivals in general. It is only after this digression that he returns to his own problem and pictures himself slipping unharmed through the darkened streets and arriving at a door which Delia opens for him, beckoning him with a snap of her fingers. He then pictures them reunited, a vision which brings him up short. What if he, if they are seen? It doesn't matter, he tells himself. He has, after all,

11

consulted a witch, who has assured him that his rival has been prevented from suspecting him by a spell she invoked.

The poet has struggled to picture each stage of his strategy in spite of his tipsiness, but the thought of the witch distracts him and soon takes control of his wandering wits. He rambles on in fact, marveling at her powers. She can bring stars down from the sky, call the dead from their graves and brew the poisons which Medea, the famous sorceress and wife of Jason, once brewed. She can even make the hounds of Hecate, the Queen of Hell, obey her. He continues in this manner, reminding his listeners of the spell the witch gave him until, suddenly, a sobering thought strikes him. Why should he believe this woman? Wasn't it she who told him that she would cure his love or, as he himself wished, make Delia return his affection and bring about the fulfillment of his dream of rural bliss? None of this has, however, been accomplished. Well, probably not the witch's fault after all, he admits. He himself has no doubt committed some sacrilege against Venus for which he is now going to have to make amends by humbling himself before the power of the goddess.

All at once his drinking companion laughs at his story, and the poet turns on him with the double fury of a drunk and a rejected lover. He warns the man who mocks him that his time will come and tells a chilling story of a man who mocked love in his younger days only to be made a fool of by love when he grew old. The poet concludes with the boast that he is not such a man. He serves Venus and asks only that she help him in return.

Translation

Pour me more wine.
No water please; pure grape
To put to rest these late-come miseries,
So sleep can seize these eyelids
That surrender as I droop.   5
No one shake me, head all banged with wine,
While poor, unhappy love lies resting here.

They've put out guards,
My darling's vicious guards,
And shut her door up tight   10

And shoved a heavy bolt across.
You, stubborn husband's door,
I hope the rain lashes at your face,
Hope bolts of lightning sent by Jove,
Will flash their way to you.   15

But door, give in to my complaint
And open - just for me. And when you do,
Play thief. No noise as hinges turn;
And if my madness has maligned you
In the past, forgive me now.   20
Let this, I beg, rest on my head.
Far better that you think of all
The promises I made as pilgrim
When I draped love's portal
With flowers that my fingers wove.   25
And Delia, you, you too, no shrinking now.
Just give your guards the slip. You must be bold.
Venus gives the brave her help, you know.
She's at his side when some man
Makes a new approach, or when a girl   30
Unlocks her gate, tooth grinding tooth
As key turns lock. She teaches them
To creep in stealth from cushioned beds;
She teaches them to plant their steps
Without a sound; she teaches them,   35
With husbands at their sides, to speak
Through little movements of their heads
And with their made-up signs to hide
The diction of their love.
She doesn't teach just anyone;   40
No, never those whom laziness makes late
Or those whom fear dissuades
From rising on a starless night.
But look at me: I wander round the city
After dark, love-sick, go anywhere and yet   45
                     *****
She lets no man approach, no man
Who'd stab me with his blade

Or try to steal my clothing just to sell.
The man whom love embraces goes
In safety anywhere, is holy and,   50
As should be, has no fear
That traps are laid for him.
The numbing cold of winter nights
Can do no harm to me, no harm
When storms throw water down in sheets.   55
Even this, this love work, brings no hurt,
As long as Delia opens up her door
And, silent, calls me with a finger's snap.

Now, turn your eyes,
You, man or woman, passing by,   60
For Venus wants her secret deed kept dark.
Don't terrify me with your tread.
Don't ask my name. Don't bring the light
Of glowing torches near.
And if some careless fool should see.   65
Let him hold his tongue and swear
By all the gods he can't recall
Just what he saw. For he who tells my tale
Will feel in time that Love's the child
Of bloodshed and the foam-wild sea.   70
But even if the fool should speak,
Your husband won't believe him, no. The witch,
True witch, has promised magic ministry.

I've seen her bring the stars down from the skies,
Reverse the course of rushing rivers with her chant.   75
She splits the soil with songs and draws
The ghosts out of their graves, then charms
The bones off glowing funeral pyres.
Sometimes she holds the crowd of dead
Unmoving with a witch's shriek   80
Or sprinkles them with milk and sends
Them back to Hell. At will, she drives
The clouds themselves out of the murky sky.
At will she marshals snow on summer gales,

The only one, they say, who knows   85
Medea's deadly drugs, the only one
To master Hecate's savage hounds.
She made this spell for me.

With this you can deceive.
Chant it three times.   90
Then spit three times when chanting's done,
And husband trusts no story told of us.
He'll not believe himself,
If he should find us in his bed.
Just keep away from other men,   95
For all the rest he'll see. Of me
And me alone he'll have no clue.

But wait. Should I believe her,
The very one who said that she
Could set me free of love with drugs and charms,   100
Who cleansed me with a flaming torch,
Who made, one moon-still night, a sacrifice
Of some dark victim to the magic powers?
I didn't ask release from all my love
But that it be returned by you.   105
I surely would not ask for the power to live
Deprived of you. He'd have to be
An iron man, who, when you could be his,
Would choose, the fool, to live
A soldier's life and pass his days   110
In ravishing the land. It's fine for him
To drive Cilicians in a rout,
To set his camp upon some captured soil,
All framed in silver, framed in gold,
A sight to see, seated high   115
Upon a galloping stallion's back.

If only, Delia, I could be with you,
I'd yoke my oxen, send my sheep myself
To pasture on the same old hill.
If only I could hold you gently in my arms,   120

loves inebriation / Softer than that / of the wine "soft as / opposed / sense?

Then softly sleep would come to me
Upon a rough and thorny patch of earth.
Why sleep upon a quilt of ruby dye
If love's denied and night comes on
With tears and wakefulness?   125
No feather pillows in that hour.
No bright embroidery, no sound
Of gently falling water then
Can bring you sleep.

I wonder. Did my words somehow insult   130
The majesty of Love?
I wonder. Do I pay the price
For a blaspheming tongue?
I wonder if they say I went
Unclean before the gods   135
Or snatched the chains of flowers
From their holy altar fires?
Well, if a penalty's deserved
I surely know my course:
To kneel before the temple   140
And place kisses on its hallowed sill,
Repentant, creep across its floor
Upon my knees and dash my head,
Unhappy head, against its holy frame.

You there, who make a joke   145
Of my unhappy state,
Untouched by grief yourself,
Look out! Your turn is next
The goddess does not keep her wrath
Forever for one man.   150
Yes, I have seen another
Mock young lovers in their hopeless love,
Have seen him, aged, bend his neck
Beneath the chains of love,
Have heard his trembling voice compose   155
Sweet nothings for a girl,
Have watched his sad attempts to keep

His silver hair in place. No shame he had,
But stood all day before his darling's door
Or tried to stop her servant   160
As she crossed the market square.
The boys pushed hard around him then,
The little boys and village toughs
Who run in roving packs;
And each spat for himself upon   165
The smooth flesh of his breast,
To keep the omen off.

But spare me, Lady Venus, please.
In mind and heart I'll always be
Your dedicated slave.   170
What use, in spite, to burn the crop
That you yourself have sown?

Commentary

Although this elegy seems, at first reading, to be merely a drunken lament, diffuse and randomly organized, it is in fact constructed with great art and subtlety. Although it contains some elements of a *komos* or song of revelry, it is, in essence, what the ancients called a *paraclausithyron*, a song sung by a lover excluded by his mistress. It is not surprising, therefore, that the two principal themes of the elegy are Venus, the goddess of love and doors, along with all the apparatus that surrounds them. More surprising is the clever manner in which Tibullus develops these themes on several levels: Venus is both the goddess of love in the abstract and the passion and lovemaking of the lovers themselves; and the doors in the poem are not only the entrances to houses and temples, but, figuratively, access to the mistress and her body as well. The poet's references to lovers' catch-words and secret codes suggests that he and his mistress are meant to be seen as employing such terms in an ambiguous way, and it is difficult to imagine that the double-meanings in this poem were not part of the code they themselves employed. In short, the reader must understand references to Venus and the poet's treatment of her as part of a code that signifies the lovers' passion and the acts it motivates.

Keeping in mind the fact that this elegy will move on these two levels of meaning, let us examine its structure with greater care. As we have seen in the Introduction, it is built in ring form. The poet's central rambling complaint is bracketed by two brief passages which describe what is actually happening at the drinking party. In the first, the poet calls to his drinking companion for more wine and orders him to leave him alone so that he may sleep. It is a passage in which he is seen making good use of the human harvest of grapes in order to alleviate the pain which his present problem has brought him. In the last passage in the poem, the poet shouts at his companion again, this time to stop his laughter and to warn the man of the fickleness of love and the vindictiveness of Venus. Then, the poem ends with a prayer to the goddess to spare the poet, and its final lines cleverly suggest that Venus is in danger of doing the very opposite of what the poet himself was seen doing as the poem opened: she may burn his love, a crop which she herself has sown.

Between these two scenes, three parts of the poet's lament may be identified. The first deals with the poet's immediate problem: how to achieve a reunion with Delia from whose presence he has been excluded. The steps by which he sees this reunion being achieved are reviewed in the poet's imagination, and as the imaginary vision of reunion unfolds, Venus herself emerges as the key to the solution of his problem. At this point she is seen as teacher and protectress, an almost proper divinity whom the poet may worship in her official shrines and upon whom he can rely to work his reconciliation

As we reach the second part of his lament, however, Venus fades away and is replaced by a more sinister power, a witch who communes with infernal forces, who solves problems by using magical, primitive, dark and unsanctioned methods. She employs chants which are accompanied at times by ritual spitting, she employs poisons, kills dark victims and turns nature itself upside down. She is, in short, the very antithesis of the bright and serene goddess Venus.

In his stupor the poet is tempted to place his trust in this witch and her craft, but he is brought up short by doubt, and as this occurs we learn why he consulted the witch in the first place. The problem presented in the poem thus far is not in fact peculiar to a single night. The poet's love affair has not been going well for some time. Venus has not in fact aided him, has not shown herself as a bright and protecting divinity, and for this reason he has gone to the witch for assistance. Thus, this passage provides a bridge from the specific problem of a single night to the more general problem: the poet's inability to gain access to Delia for a considerable period of time.

At the beginning of the third part of the central portion of the elegy, we find a restatement of what the poet's broad and long-range wishes are. This comes in the form of an echo of the preceding elegy, and it is introduced by the poet's reference to the hard heart of any man who would choose to live without Delia for the sake of gain. This thought leads in turn to the contrast between the earlier poem's adventurer, who denies himself love's delight for the sake of glory and gain, and the poet, who desires only simple country pleasures and the love of his mistress.

But the poet's desires are not being fulfilled, not tonight, not any night, and so he searches further for the reason for this, returning once more to Venus and recalling his earlier treatment of her. He has already hinted at some guilt of his own in the first part of his lament where he made reference to the mistreatment of the door. And here too, although the affront appears to be to Venus, her temple and its door are clearly mentioned. The poet suggests that he may have stolen flowers from the temple and promises to make amends by crawling to the door and beating his head against it. Significantly, it is at this very point, as the poet's word play grows more humorous and suggestive, that one of his companions laughs at him, a taunt which brings him and us back to the reality of the drinking scene and away from his rambling lament and imaginary stratagems.

In the brief closing scene which follows Tibullus recapitulates his main themes; the harshness and fickleness of Venus, the temptation to use magic (the little boys spit to keep an evil omen away just as the witch taught him to spit when reciting her charm.), and finally, his own willingness to be Venus' slave. We should take note as well that Tibullus cleverly concludes with a powerful image of an elderly lover, an image that looks back to the themes of the preceding elegy and provides at the same time justification for the poet's insistence on the pursuit in youth of amatory delights, of all that Venus, whatever that name signifies here, can bestow on him.

✦   ✦   ✦

1.3

Introduction

The poet lies ill on an island, probably Corfu, which he refers to in this poem by a form of the name Homer used of its people, Phaeacia. He has, we are told, set out with his patron Messalla on a campaign to the East, a kind of latter-day Odysseus who because of illness has been left behind on the island by the rest of the expeditionary force. We are not told the precise nature of his affliction but everything we learn about it suggests that it is serious. The forsaking of the expedition and the poet's obsession with death indicate this, as does the very form of the poem, which presents the rambling thoughts of a mind seemingly altered by sickness.

In this elegy, it appears, Tibullus has devised yet another mental frame, another literary alteration of consciousness, and through this lens of sickness and suffering the poems's seemingly random transitions achieve greater verisimilitude. The geographical and literary location of the poem is also important. Homer's Phaeacia was a land of wonders, suspended between the real world and the world of fantasy, not far, significantly, from Elysium, which is described later in the elegy. The poet finds himself in just such a world not only because of the altered state of his mind but also because he is between the very real world of Messalla, the practical commander and man of the world, and the imagined world of Delia whom he has left behind in Rome.

The poem opens with a brief reference to Messalla's world and with the hope that the poet will be remembered by those who have left him on the island. But the poet then turns at once to his central obsession: the thought of death and especially of a lonely death in a strange place. Lamenting the absence of those he loves from his imagined funeral, the poet thinks of Delia and those thoughts make him remember his departure from her, her fears, his hesitation and the omens which the gods sent at the moment of their parting.

21

Gods and omens - these in turn evoke an image of Delia taking part in her favorite form of worship, the celebration of Isis, the Egyptian goddess whose cult had grown so popular among Roman women during the first century. Isis was a fertility goddess whose brother Osirus had been murdered and then brought back to life with the help of Isis' son Horus, the sun god. Like the ceremonies of other cults, worship of Isis included ritual purification and, as the poet tells us here, offered the promise of miraculous cures. So it is that he quite naturally recalls the rituals which Delia performed in the past and, thinking of them, cries out for the goddess' help in his present illness, offering her the promise of Delia's continued worship at her shrines, one of the greatest of which, that on the island of Pharos, is alluded to here.

The thought of Delia's favorite but very un-Roman goddess makes the poet think of his own special divinities, the Lares and Penates, who were the protectors of a Roman house. In turn, their recollection summons thoughts of still older divinities, of Saturn, the father of Jupiter and of the golden age over which he ruled. The poet's muddled brain dwells for sometime on the simple goodness and unsophisticated pleasures of that distant age, themes which, as we have noted in earlier poems, reflect his own yearning for a life of uncomplicated rural piety and delight. He reminds himself, however, that the age of Saturn did not endure. Saturn was overthrown by his son Jupiter, who brought in an age of human greed and arrogance, of anger and of war, an age which has in fact sent the poet himself on the military campaign which has made him ill and might yet result in his death.

At this point he is brought up short. What if he does in fact die? Is he even now blaspheming in speaking in this way about Jupiter and his reign? No, he reassures himself, there is nothing to fear. He has always treated the gods with respect, and therefore, if he dies, his gravestone will put his death down to the perils of war alone, and his soul will go to Elysium, that paradise of lovers, where there is music and dancing and where throngs of young lovers enjoy an idyllic eternity. The fevered brain of the poet dwells upon this bright vision but only briefly, for in a moment it focuses on the opposite place, the gloomy plain of Tartarus which is reserved for the wicked, for those who, in the poet's view, have violated love. This is the underworld of dark anguish and suffering, guarded by monsters like Tisiphone with her serpent hair and the watchdog Cerberus. In this place sinners are tortured: Ixion lashed to a spinning wheel, Tityos feeding birds upon his bowels, Tantalus ever thirsty but unable to drink, and the unfaithful daughters of Danaus, who are condemned for the wedding-night murder of their husbands to carry forever the waters of Lethe, the river of forgetfulness, in jars that leak.

And so the chain of rambling associations continues. The visions of Hell make the poet think of those who deserve Hell, among them his wealthy rival in Rome, who represents the greatest threat to Delia's fidelity and who, in all likelihood, prays for the poet's continued absence. He refuses to accept this outcome, however, and, still delirious, imagines himself in the role of Odysseus, dreaming of Delia as if she were another chaste and steadfast Penelope at home with her maids, sewing and listening to the tales they tell. And he sees himself returning but, unlike Odysseus, reappearing suddenly at Delia's door. Delia, less reserved than Homer's Penelope, runs to greet him half-dressed. We are struck by her disarray. Is she Penelope after all? Has the poet's muddled brain allowed his worst fears to seep into his vision of bliss? Where, we wonder, is the rival in this moment of sudden return? This doubt does not, however, reach the poet's own consciousness. He gives himself up to the bright vision of their early morning reunion. The poem which began with imagined death ends, for him, with imagined joy. Is either vision true? Who can tell? We are after all on Phaeacia in an unreal world of dream and fantasy to which the poet has fled, the only world in which, it seems, a failed Odysseus can find fulfillment.

Translation

You'll go without me
Over the Aegean Sea.
I only hope, Messalla, you
And all your fellows hold me in your thoughts:
Me, Phaeacia's captive, ailing   5
In a land of strangers, no place to die.
So Death, black Death,
Keep greedy hands away. That's what I ask.
No mother here to clutch charred bones
Against a grief-scarred breast,   10
No sister who can pour perfumes
From Syria upon my ash,
With streaming hair weep warmly at my grave.

No Delia here.

Before she sent me on my way from Rome　　　15
She made the rounds, they say, of all the gods
To get their views. Three times she picked
The sacred lots the acolyte held out,
And he three times reported every omen clear:
All granted my return.　　　　　　　　　　20
And yet she would not quench her tears,
Stop fretting over my plans to sail;
And even I, her consolation,
When I'd given the last commands,
Heart-sick, still sought reasons for delay.　　25
The birds were my excuses then,
Or omens or the sabbath day.
How many times when I had started off
I called my tripping at the door
An evil sign! When Love's against him,　　30
Let no man dare to leave,
Or, leaving he will learn too soon
He left against the god's commands.

What good's your Isis, Delia, now?
What good to me those times you clapped　　35
The rattle's brass upon your palm?
What good the times you carried out
Her rites, devout? What good -
I still remember now -
To purify yourself, to bathe,　　　　　　　40
To sleep alone in a bed unstained?
Now is the time for help.
O goddess, help me now,
For all those temple pictures teach
That you can cure.   Help me, I pray!　　45
Then Delia, making good her vow,
Can sit before your temple doors.
In linen twice a day, with hair let down,
A stand-out in that Pharian crowd,
Sing hymns in praise of you.　　　　　　50

But as for me -
I only want to worship the gods
Who watched my father's house,
And month by month give incense
To our household's ancient powers divine.   55
How well they lived when Saturn was our lord,
Before the earth lay naked
To the ploughing of our keels.   *No war -*
No ship had yet defied the deep-blue sea
And turned its pouting sail to catch the wind.   60
No sailor, wandering in uncharted realms,
For profit let his ship ride low
With foreign goods. Those days the sturdy bull
Endured no yoke. No horse bit bridle,
His mouth no longer wild.   65
The houses had no doors, no stone was placed
In fields to mark the boundaries of the land.
The oaks gave honey then.
Uncalled, the ewes brought udders full of milk,
A gift to carefree shepherds - then.   70
No charging lines of infantry,
No wrath then and no wars.
No savage smith had yet produced a sword
With skill - but no humanity.

Now Jupiter is lord,   75
And we have slaughter always, always wounded men.
And now we have the sea to sail
And now a thousand other roads
That run to sudden death.
But Father, spare us, for no perjury   80
Brings terror to my cowardly heart,
No blasphemy I spoke
Against the sacred gods. Still, even now,
If I have had my fill of fated years,
Then let them place a stone upon my bones   85
And let its message read:
"Here lies Tibullus, swallowed
By a death that came too soon

While following Messalla on the land and sea."
Because I always gave, and gracefully,   90
To tender Love her due, Venus herself
Will lead me to Elysium and its fields
That are alive with song, alive with dance,
Where, here and there, the wandering birds
Set slender throats aquiver with sweet song.   95
Uncared for, nature cinnamons her fields,
And meadow after meadow there
The kindly earth's abloom with fragrant rose;
There lines of boys romp hand-in-hand
With graceful girls, love always at their sides   100
To prompt their battles and their mingling.
This is the place where lovers go
When greedy death has come; and there
Each wears a garland made of myrtle leaves
As crown upon his hair.   105

But hidden in a night profound,
The home of the accursed lies;
And round about it pitch-black rivers roar.
Tisiphone, a horror, rages there,
Wild snakes for hair in tangled disarray.   110
This way and that she drives
The crowd of guilty souls in flight;
And Cerberus, all black,
Sits hissing at the gate with serpents' mouths,
A crouching guard before the doors of bronze.   115
There Ixion, who plotted Juno's rape,
Whirls round and round, his guilty arms
And legs chained upon a speeding wheel;
And Tityos lies stretched across
Nine acres of the land and feeds   120
And feeds the constant birds
Upon his black and bleeding bowels.
There's Tantalus, the water at his chin,
Which, when he'd drink, deserts his pinching thirst;
And Danaus' daughters, who for harm   125
To Venus' power bear Lethe's water

In their leaking jars. Your place
Whoever violates my love
And wishes me a long campaign.

[handwritten marginalia: is he condemning the wealth roman the... 130]

But Delia, please live chaste.
Steadfast, I beg you, always keep
That conscientious hag right at your side
To guard your virtue, telling tales
By lamplight, drawing strands of wool
From an unused spool, while at her side,   135
Bent to aching toil, the drowsy girls
Droop one by one to sleep and drop their work.

[handwritten marginalia: Penelope]

That moment I might suddenly come.
No announcement made, appear
Before you as if heaven-sent;   140
And then, just as you are, long curls uncombed,
Run, barefoot, Delia, to my side.
This is what I pray: let brilliant dawn
On rosy horses, bring that hour to us,
That Lucifer, that shining morning star.   145

Commentary

[handwritten note: morning star, star that brings light.]

The superficial structure of this elegy outlined in the introduction
above is based upon the illusion that the poet is speaking from his
sickbed in a state of feverish delirium. Beneath this structure, however,
we can discern yet another design which is not linear but graphically
arranged, not temporal or mental but achieved through the disposition of
sensual images and recurring themes in the text.

At the center of this deeper structure is the poem's most prominent
image and theme: death. It is inscribed in the poet's own statement of
his willingness to die and, even more strikingly in his vision of his own
tombstone and the composition of his epitaph. This central vision of the
poet's own death is bracketed by two sets of contrasts. Before it in the
text Tibullus has placed a contrast between the age of Saturn and the age
of Jupiter; after it lies a contrast between the two kinds of fate that await
souls after death, the blissful happiness of Elysium, significantly Saturn's
realm, and the suffering and torture of Tartarus. These two sets of

contrasts are closely related. The age of Saturn represents the poet's ideal of rural simplicity and unsophisticated happiness; the age of Jupiter, the false ideal of the contemporary man, of all those, who like the poet's rival, live to acquire wealth and power. Death which comes between the two sets of contrasts in the text acts as mediator. It is often brought about by the false values current in Jupiter's age, it is true, but, as this design emphasizes, it also brings to each soul the afterlife it has deserved. He who lives the simple life is brought, as the following set of contrasts illustrates, to Elysium; the sinner is condemned to pay for his sin in Tartarus.

This central tripartite core of the poem, the presentation of death bracketed by corresponding contrasts, is timeless, for it lies beyond the imagined temporal world of the poem. It presents a religious and moral statement about life and ethical values, about death and about the relation of all of these things to eternity. This portion of the elegy is in turn bracketed by two outer segments which are, quite the contrary, based in time. One of these, that with which the poem opens deals with present, past and future, with the poet's present sickness in a forsaken land, with his departure from Rome in the recent past and with the rituals Delia observed at that time, and finally with the future, viewed in two ways: as death, if his prayers are not answered, and as a life of fulfillment if they are. The second outer frame comes at the end of the poem and is likewise based in time, first in the present and then suddenly in the future, an imagined future that envisions the poet's return to his mistress. In this frame Delia is imagined as the faithful Penelope with whom the poet is reunited in answer to his prayer.

Viewed graphically, then, the poem contains a timeless tripartite central core which is bracketed by two time-bound outer frames. The only certainty in the poem lies at its core: death. On either side of it lie the realms of moral choice and the results of that choice in the life to come. At the periphery lie the realms of the greatest uncertainty, the realms of time, of individual fate and action. In the first of these two frames, which presents the beginning of the linear narrative, the uncertainty is explicitly stated: the poet may live or he may die. In the second the uncertainty is denied by the poet, at least in the fantasy in which he indulges, and remains implicit for the reader: Delia may be chaste, sitting night after night with her maids like a latter-day Penelope, or then again she may betray the poet. Even in his imagination, when she runs to meet him, hair in disarray, as the poem draws to a close, who can know with certainty from what other bed she has come?

In short, at the periphery of this elegy we find the frequent Tibullan theme of the instability of human affairs and of the corresponding uncertainty that characterizes human thinking and feeling. These themes account for the prominence of religion, ritual and magic in his poetry. In that outer realm of change and doubt one needs to use every possible means to gain one's ends: one draws lots, says prayers, watches omens, even worships, if necessary, strange gods. Better still, according to our poet, one lives by the precepts of the old Roman religion, which remains, he believes, man's surest guide in an unreliable world.

The graphic structure of this elegy permits, we should also note, the ingenious use of yet another of Tibullus' favorite poetic devices, the recurrence of a single image in varying contexts to produce varying effects. The image with which the poet seems to be obsessed in this poem, as he is in others as well, is hair, and the obsession is skillfully employed. In the first of the outer frames flowing hair is linked to each of the possible outcomes of the poet's prayers: a sister's flowing hair whose absence from his funeral the poet laments, and Delia's flowing hair as she offers thanksgiving for the poet's recovered health. Likewise, in the poem's subsequent vision of life after death the serpent locks of Tisiphone stand in contrast to the lover's hair that is crowned with myrtle in Elysium. And in the final frame, in which the poet imagines his reunion with Delia, her own uncombed hair becomes the very symbol of the ambiguity with which the poem closes. Is Delia's flowing hair an indication of her eagerness to see the poet, of her grief over his absence, or of her recent dalliance with another lover? Tibullus leaves this question unanswered but indicates by the use of this recurring image at this crucial moment that it surely must be posed.

✦   ✦   ✦

1.4

Introduction

The poet is engaged in conversation with a statue. He is in a garden in which he has come upon the wooden figure of Priapus, naked and adorned, as was customary, with a large erect phallus. Priapus was in fact the protector of Roman gardens but was also known as the helper of lovers and the advisor of the love-lorn. When the poet meets the god's effigy, he gives it a proper greeting and then asks what it is that makes Priapus so popular with handsome boys. Priapus is not, he notes, especially handsome himself. Could it be, the poet wonders, that it is the cleverness and wit of the god that attracts young men?

The statue does not really answer the question and we are left to guess for ourselves what it is that attracts the young men's attention and admiration. Instead of replying to the poet's question Priapus begins a long and formal lecture on pederasty. It is organized with care and couched in a lofty didactic style. Filled with clever allusions and wise aphorisms, it has an oracular quality.

The god begins by imploring the poet to put no trust in boys, but then, quite abruptly, he betrays his real feelings by describing their varieties and many attractions. How he enjoys picturing the young equestrian, the swimmer, one boy who is bold, another who is shy! And then, continuing his lecture, he reflects upon how patient a pederast must be, comparing the pursuit of young men to the taming of lions or the wearing away of rocks by running water, to the ripening of grapes and even to the revolution of the stars. Such love is not merely seasonal, he proclaims, but cosmic, and it is, therefore, above the law. One can swear to a youthful lover and break one's oath with impunity. Jupiter

31

himself permits this just as he permitted Diana, here referred to as
Dictynna, the Cretan nymph, and Minerva, the goddess of household
crafts, to swear falsely without fear of punishment.

On the other hand, the god counsels against procrastination. He
meditates in passing on the swift passage of time and the inevitable
advance of old age. Only Bacchus, the god of wine, and Apollo enjoy
perpetual youth and can, therefore, wear their hair uncut forever. Men,
however, must grow old, must cut their hair when they reach manhood
and live in time to regret their missed opportunities. The pederast must
be patient but not dilatory.

What else must a lover do? Anything his beloved wants, Priapus
advises, proceeding at once to list the activities that must be endured:
long journeys even in the rain, sailing, hunting and fencing, the last a
pastime in the course of which the lover must even allow himself to be
bested by his lover. Priapus admits, however, that even the willingness
to endure all of this does not assure success. This, he adds, is because
young men have been corrupted by the present age, which has taught
them to expect gifts and payment for their favors. Priapus curses the
evil man who introduced such innovations and begins to lecture the
young men themselves. They should, he tells them, love poets and the
Muses, for they confer not material gifts but immortality. He pauses at
this point to demonstrate the poet's power to immortalize with several
examples of legendary heroes made famous in verse: King Nisus of
Megara, whose sister betrayed her native city by cutting his hair, and
Pelops whose father, Tantalus, killed and cooked him, but whose
shoulder, after having been eaten by Demeter, was refashioned out of
ivory. The wooden god ends his lecture by extending his curse to all who
show no respect for poetic gifts. May these boys, he prays, become
galli, the castrated priests of the Phrygian goddess Cybele, who danced
around her cart-born shrine to a tune piped by flute players.

When Priapus falls silent, the poet himself assumes the role of teacher,
giving the impression that, although he is above the practice of
pederasty, he is nevertheless willing to pass the god's advice along to
others. He will give it, for example, to his friend Titius, and if Titius'
wife won't let him listen, well then he will offer his lessons to the public
at large and even become well known for his pedagogy.

Then, suddenly, only a few lines from the end of the poem, he cries
out in anguish. He too, we learn, is being tortured by a reluctant
beloved, a boy whose name is Marathus. He can dissemble no longer;

he is mad for the boy and admits at last that, if his love is not returned, his public profession of wisdom will make him the laughing stock of Rome.

Translation

       "I pray, Priapus, that you always have
       This roof of shade, so suns won't burn your head,
       No snows do harm, wondering as I pray
       What cleverness of yours beguiles the pretty boys.
       You have no shining beard, no hair   5
       All primped with every curl in place,
       But naked, drudge the long days
       Of stormy winter's frost,
       And naked too, endure
       The Dog star's thirsty skies."   10

       That's what I said,
       And bristling with his crescent pruning hook,
       Bacchus' hayseed child replied,
       "I beg you, sir, don't fall into the hands
       Of sweet-fleshed boys. You know the crowd: 15
       Each one with prompting for your proper love:
       This one because he's master of his mount
       And never lets the reins go slack;
       This one because his snow-white chest
       Can cleave the glassy stillness of a pool.   20
       And this one has your heart
       Because he's bold and brave,
       This one because a virgin blush
       Plays winsome warden on his tender cheek.

       But if it happens that one turns   25
       You down at first, don't take it hard;
       For, bit by bit, he'll bend his neck
       Beneath your yoke. It took long days
       When men taught lions to obey.
       Long days must pass before the gentle stream   30
       Can wear the stones away.

A year's required to ripen grapes
Upon a sun-drenched hill; a year
To bring the brilliant star signs
Around the zodiac on time.   35
Don't be afraid to take an oath.
Love's perjuries the winds pick up,
Drive off unsanctioned, land and sea.
Give thanks to mighty Jupiter,
Our father, who decreed   40
That nothing sworn by fools in love
Would have the slightest weight.
For he allowed Dictynna,
Swearing falsely by her shafts,
Minerva, by her curls, to go unpunished both.   45

But wait too long and then you're lost.
Youth's gone! There are no sluggish days.
How quickly they are here, depart.
How quickly lost the summer blush of earth's brief bloom.
How quickly towering poplars shed their lovely hair.   50
The horse that used to bolt in front,
The first out of Olympia's gate,
How low it lies when fated, feeble age has come.
I've seen myself young men
Who lived to grieve for days   55
They foolishly allowed to pass
When later years had bent them down with age.
The gods are cruel. The serpent
Is renewed and sheds his years,
But fate gives beauty not an hour to tarry in.   60
On Bacchus and Apollo and on them alone
Perpetual youth has been bestowed:
Both gods with grace may let their hair grow long.

But you, whatever deed
Your darling boy would like to try,   65
Give him his way.
Love wins the most by giving in,
So don't refuse to go along

However far the journey seems,
However hot the Dog star burns 70
The fields with parching thirst.
'Though rainbow, stormbow veils
The showers sure to come and daubs
The sky with strokes of iron gray,
Even then, should he dash off to ply 75
Blue waters in his boat,
Pick up the oars yourself
And drive the skiff across the waves.
And no regrets for you,
In taking up the heavy task, 80
In calluses on hands unused to toil.
Or if he wants to ring
The mountain passes with his traps,
Your shoulders then must not refuse
To carry nets. And if it's off 85
To fencing, parry with a blunted stroke
And often turn your open side for him to stab.
Then he'll be pliant, he'll be mild;
And you can take a lover's golden kiss.
He'll fight, but when it's stolen, 90
Yield it, lip to lip, give first
What's stolen - then offer it himself
On your demand, offer perhaps at last
To twine himself, unasked, around your neck.

But O, it's foul the way our age 95
Traffics in these sickening arts, for now
Young men grow used to getting gifts for love.
You there, who first taught love to sell itself,
I hope, whoever you may be,
A luckless stone lies heavy on your bones. 100
It's learned poets you should love, sweet boys,
Poets and the graceful Muse;
And let no gift of gold outbid the Muse.
In song the hair of Nisus has a purple hue,
And if no song were sung, 105
No flash of ivory on old Pelop's back.

Yes, he, the subject of the Muse's song,
Will live as long as earth bears trees
The sky its stars, as long as rivers run;
But he who turns deaf ears upon the Muse   110
And sells his love, may he be doomed
To trail behind the cars
Of eastern Cybele and her crowd,
Wandering, fill a list of thrice a hundred towns
And to a Phrygian tune castrate   115
The member that he sold so cheap.
Yes, Venus wants a place for sweet conceits
Of love and favors plaintiff lovers' prayers
And blesses sad, sad tears."
These things the god intoned for me;   120
And I would like to pass them on
To Titius in my song, if Titius' wife
Would not forbid his calling them to mind.
Well let him heed his wife.
But you who suffer at the hands   125
Of shrewd and guileful boys, flock all to me
And celebrate my teaching skill.
Each man has a glory all his own.
Spurned lovers in the days to come
Will visit me and find my door   130
Is open wide. The time will come
When doting crowds of younger men
Will follow me to town
As I, grown old, pronounce
The precepts of their love.   135

But god, Marathus! How he twists me,
Tortures with his halting love.
No power in my skill;
No power in my strategies.
Have pity, boy, I pray,   140
For I would rather not become
Some dirty piece of gossip, no,
With gusts of laughter echoing
To mock the hollow wisdom I bestow.

Commentary

This elegy is a mock didactic poem, a poem which teaches but with tongue in cheek. It is this, but it is something more as well, as an analysis of its structure will reveal. One of its most striking characteristics is the manner in which a superficial symmetry masks its essentially asymmetrical design. Consider first the apparent symmetry, which is easily discerned in both the poem as a whole and in its parts. First, the entire elegy is divided into three distinct sections: the opening in which the poet addresses the statue of Priapus, the long central portion in which the statue delivers his lecture and the closing passage in which the poet reflects upon the lecture and considers its meaning for him. Superficially then, the poem has the form of a lecture, preceded by an introduction and followed by a reaction, both of these delivered by the poet who acts as the moderator of the proceedings.

The central lecture is also carefully designed and contains a neatly arranged series of reflections and admonitions which delineate the uncertainties of the pederast's world and the anxieties these generate, along with strategies for responding to these challenges. The tone is largely didactic and sober, but a plaintiff note insinuates itself into the instruction from time to time, a note intended, I believe, to puzzle the reader and arouse his suspicions about the true source of this piece of advice to lovers of young men. Even these plaintiff intrusions, however, cannot mar the carefully balanced design of the individual parts of the speech. Note, for example, how the attractions of the young men that are enumerated early in the speech respond to one another: the first two are physical, the last two mental or emotional. The first physical attraction involves restraint as does the last mental one, shyness on one level echoing poised horsemanship on the other. Between these, two active, almost violent attractions make their appearance: swimming on one level, boldness and daring on the other.

The examples of the lover's patient endurance are arranged with the same care. They move from human to animal behavior, then to natural phenomena, to seasonal or cyclic activity and finally to cosmic movement. As the scale of these activities grows larger so too does the time span required for their fulfillment, so that the structure of this part of the poem moves in a crescendo of both magnitude and time. The treatment of passing youth and beauty begins with a catalogue of examples arranged in a similar ascending order: first plant life, then animal life and finally human life. These are then capped by a cry of complaint against the gods. And again, Priapus' lesson is driven home by contrasts between the fleeting nature of human beauty first with the beauty of a lower form of life, the serpent, and then with a higher form, the gods Bacchus and Apollo. The lesson's final catalogue deals with the beloved's favorite activities. It too forms a crescendo, beginning as it does with activities that involve only moderate exertions and risk and proceeding to more strenuous pastimes like hunting and finally to violent sport which involves the risk of physical injury.

The central part of the elegy, the speech of Priapus, may also be viewed as an ingeniously designed play of images and time. The images are arranged in climactic categories but they are also affected and thus ordered by time. The lover's resistance and those images which symbolize it are worn down by time. On the other hand, human beauty, unlike its opposites, fades under the influence of time and therefore, time becomes in yet another way the most crucial factor in the lover's struggle. Finally, the importance of time is artfully emphasized in the images of the beloved's grudging yielding of a stolen kiss, which time changes into the kiss which he himself demands.

If time represents the force that reorders by bringing change, recurring images represent what is unchanging. For example,"hair" occurs again and again as a symbol of enduring beauty or of its opposite, ugliness, and images drawn from the world of natural phenomena, heat, cold, storms and burning sun are presented as correlatives for the obstacles that the determined lover must overcome and for those abiding negative forces that can wear down even the wise god himself.

In spite of this superficial balance and symmetry, however, the elegy is essential asymmetrical, and we should not be misled by the artistry of the parody which necessarily mimics the techniques of the parodied genre. The poem is asymmetrical because its meaning is withheld from the reader until its final lines. Until that point the poem moves in ambiguity and mystery. Why, we ask ourselves at first reading, are we being given this elaborate parody, this comic talking statue? As the statue lectures us, we find ourselves in the position of someone hearing a long and tedious joke. Only the statue's tendency to lament arouses our suspicions and signals to us that something else may be going on, that we had better read further.

And so it is that when the statue finishes his lecture, we are eager to hear more from the poet. And what does he tell us? That he is himself going to become a famous teacher of pederasts, since, he laments, the wives of his friends won't let them listen to what he says. This is hardly a satisfactory explanation. We feel that we have been duped yet again, taken for a literary ride by this poet who begins to see himself as the wooden teacher of pederasts. Could there be something more in this identification? Tibullus keeps this from us until the very last lines in which the truth emerges: the poet is desperately in love with a young man himself. And so Priapus and the poet are in fact one. Priapus was a surrogate and an image of the poet's sad vision of himself, the embarrassed pederast who would hide his lechery in a pompous and hypocritical dissertation on the seduction of boys, a dissertation which totters always on the edge of self-revealing lament.

This structure, which is based upon the technique of deliberate mystification and withheld meaning, reveals the true nature of the elegy. It is indeed comic and contains an excellent parody of didactic poetry, but more than that, it is a confession of self-doubt and an exercise in self mockery in which the poet reveals both his embarrassing unrequited passion and his failed attempt to disguise that passion behind a mask of professorial propriety.

✦ ✦ ✦

1.5

Introduction

The poet's love affair with Delia continues to go badly. In this elegy, another variation upon the *paraclausithyron*, he is trying to salvage his dream of love, to find in the unstable world of emotion and passion some certainty and stability, some constancy and rest. It is an attempt, as we shall see, that is doomed to failure. As the elegy begins, we discover that the poet's earlier attempts at finding a remedy for his love have failed. He told himself when he was rejected that he could live without Delia, but as his present state demonstrates, that hope was an illusion. His belief that his love would be returned out of gratitude, because it was he who tended to Delia's needs when she was mortally ill, he who saved her life, has likewise proved to be a foolish fancy. He is forced to admit at last that gratitude has no place in Delia's reckoning, for, in fact, as soon as she regained her health, she bestowed her favors on another man.

Nor can the delights of rural life, which the poet envisions in the following lines, win Delia's affection. Being the mistress of her own farm and villa holds, it seems, no attraction for her, not even when that status is enhanced by the visits of rich and powerful men like Messalla. No, the poet has had to face the fact that neither gratitude nor simple pleasure will win Delia; and so, since he cannot forget her by a simple act of the will, he has tried to find forgetfulness in yet other ways: first in wine and then in the arms of another woman. Both of these attempts, however, were doomed to failure.

Thoughts of Delia will simply not go away. Her vision, the image of her face, hovers before the poet's eyes always and his obsession with her beauty is captured here, at the center of the poem, by the image of Thetis, the daughter of the sea god Nereus, riding upon a bridled sea creature to visit Peleus her lover. This vision of the lovely sea maiden borne across the sea to her mate, is in fact a transformation of the poet's vision of his idealized Delia, a vision which, like that of Thetis, is constantly in motion and ever beyond his grasp.

The appearance of this vision coincides with the poet's realization that his attempts to find constancy in love are doomed, and these two forces, passion and disillusionment, combine to produce a fit of bitter rage in his heart. This rage is now directed against his new rival, yet another rich lover, and against the old woman who finds Delia her lovers and arranges her affairs. It is this latter figure, the crone procuress, who now bears the full force of the poet's wrath, perhaps because, as a woman, she can act as a surrogate for Delia herself. As we shall see, the current lover, although hated, is in fact doomed, in the poet's mind, to suffer the same agonies that the poet is now suffering and is, to that extent at least, a more sympathetic figure. In any case, the old woman is cursed in an elaborate and extraordinary manner. The curse calls down on her poverty, hunger, haunting and madness, and at its conclusion, the reason for its severity is made perfectly clear. This will be the payment for what the poet has suffered in being separated from his beloved. Yes, the old woman is, it seems, a surrogate for Delia, the real cause of the suffering, who as the object of the poet's love cannot be, psychologically at least, the object of his hatred.

Before the poem draws to a conclusion, the poet makes one more plea for a forlorn lover such as he. Such a lover will serve his mistress as a slave, escort her to parties with her friends, waiting upon her every wish. Will she relent then? No, his poetry is without power. His love is doomed. There is no constancy, no certainty, no stability in the world of passion. Everything moves, everything turns. Even now, he warns Delia's present lover, her next victim is outside her door, pacing back and forth, gazing up at her window.

And so the poem closes with this bitter conclusion: love is a thief that steals what we imagine we posses. Love, like much of what we consider real and reliable, changes always, like a river into which we can never step twice, a river whose undulating waters are the poem's final and striking image.

Translation

Plain mad and stubborn,
I kept saying I could stand
Your being gone. Easy. But now -
My gutsy boasting lies in distant exile,
And I am driven like a top, sent speeding   5
From its string across a level yard,
A top some boy speed demon twirls
The way he's learned a thousand afternoons.

Flame the uncouth braggart in me,
Torture me and never let me speak   10
Such pompous rot again.
Muzzle tight my barking mouth.
But all the same, forgive, forget,
By the promises of our thieving bed,
By love, by heads that lay in longing,   15
To a single pillow pledged.

I was the one, when you lay sick
With fever, almost dead, the one,
They say, who saved you with my prayers.
I went myself around your bed,   20
Performed the purifying rite
With cleansing sulphur, and when the hag
Had chanted through her magic charm,
Myself took care no nightmares did you harm,
Those fearful dreams that are dispersed   25
By the triple sprinkling of the holy crumbs.
With banded, hooded head.
And tunic falling free, nine times
I made the offering in the hush of night
To Hecate, Queen of Hell.   30

All the rites I, yes I, performed,
And now another tastes your love
And in good fortune carries off
The profit of my prayers.

Quite mad I was, imagining   35
My happy life once you were well.
But a god behind me surely shook his head.
I saw it all: how I would plough the fields,
With Delia there to watch the crops,
While threshing floor ground fine the grain   40
Beneath the blazing sun. Some days,
I told myself, she'll store the grapes
In brimming vats, some days
The new white wine that tripping feet
Have pressed. She'll learn to number flocks,   45
And little slaves in baby talk
Will learn as well to play
Upon their loving lady's lap.
She'll know what gifts to give the farmer god:
Grapes for the vines and ears of corn   50
For crops in fields, a sacrificial dinner
For the herds. She would, I told myself,
. Give everyone commands, make everything
Her care, and it would be my joy
In all the matters of the house   55
To be a cipher, unrequired on every side.
And when my friend, Messalla, came, she'd pick
The sweetest apples from her favorite trees
To honor greatness in the man.
She'd give him all her care   60
Carry out his every wish,
Herself his table's serving girl.
These scenes I used to picture to myself,
But all of these fond hopes the winds
Have taken, East and South, and sent them   65
Far beyond Armenia, that fragrant land.

How many times I've tried to drive
My cares away with wine, to find
That sorrow turned each cup to tears.
How many times I've clasped   70
Another woman to my side;
But when I came to take my joy,

Love brought my mistress to my mind
And fled. Then, as she left, the girl
Would call me cursed - the shame of it - and claim   75
My Delia practiced magic rites.
Untrue. She doesn't do it with a chant.
With face and silk-soft arms and yellow hair
My mistress casts her spell.
So, once upon a time, fair Thetis,   80
Nereus' sweet and blue-eyed child,
Sailed to visit Peleus in Thessaly
Upon a bridled dolphin's back.

These are the things that gave me pain,
And now some wealthy lover's by her side.   85
Some shrewd procuress came upon the scene
To work my doom. I hope she eats in time
A bloody meal and with her gory mouth
Drinks bitter cups all filled with gall. May ghosts
Fly round her, moaning always of their fates.   90
May shrieking owls cry violent from her roof.
Then, mad with hunger's sting, I hope
She scrapes for grass among the graves
And for the bones that savage wolves
Have left behind. Half-naked,   95
Howling, may she run throughout the town,
And may a pack of vicious dogs dispatch
Her from the crossroads where she holds her rites.
These things will come to pass; god gives me signs.
A lover has his heaven too;   100
Forsaken Venus seethes with rage
To find her covenants despised.

But as for you, my Delia, drop
The precepts that your greedy hag sets down.
Must every love be overcome by bribes?   105
Just take a poor man - always at your side -
A poor man - always first to come,
And fix himself like stave or nail
Inside the tight-fleshed softness of your side,

A poor man, steadfast guide,   110
Within a jostling crowd
Will thrust his arm before you
And make you room to walk.
A poor man, on the sly,
Will bring you to your secret friends   115
And slip the sandals from your snowy feet.

This poetry - I see it now - has no effect.
Your doors do not relent,
Will not swing open at my words,
But want a pounding by a fuller fist.   120
You there, who have her in your power for now,
Look on my fate and be afraid.
It turns, turns faster, fickle, fickle chance,
Revolving like a wheel. And not without a prize
That patient fellow stands,   125
All eyes, outside her gate
And often looks upstairs, then walks away,
Pretends to pass the house,
Then hurries back all by himself
And coughs while passing by your door.   130
Yes, thieving love is up to something new.
So take advantage while you can.
That boat of yours is swimming in a gentle stream
But one that's undulating too.

Commentary

It is not surprising to find many images of movement in a poem that
deals with instability and change in human affairs and especially in the
affairs of the heart. And indeed such images not only abound in this
elegy but are also an important structural element and perhaps the key
to its form.

The poem begins with violent and rapid movement related to childish
behavior: the image of a little boy's spinning top. This motion captures
at once the poet's state of mind and then gives way, as he contemplates
various solutions to his problem, to other kinds of motion. The first of
these is found in the slow and solemn procession around Delia's sick

bed. Then, with the return of Delia's health, the poet returns to his recurring dream of rural bliss and gives us yet another set of motions, those pertaining to everyday life and work: the crushing of grapes, the threshing of grain, the scampering of children and the serving of meals. At the center of the poem he places the hypnotic motion referred to above, the movement of Thetis, the idealized Delia, as she sails upon her dolphin to meet her lover. This vision of gentle motion does not, however, remain long before us. It is replaced by the violent and erratic movements of the cursed procuress as envisioned by the vindictive and lovelorn poet. To her own movements are added as well those of the ghosts which haunt her and the dogs which drive her from the crossroads. All of this suggests that the poet's mind has found no rest and no solution for the problem that causes his agitation. He is caught up once again in the same kind of motion with which the poem began.

Still other solutions come to his mind, however, and so, once again, the violent motion gives way to movement of a slower kind. The poet imagines himself walking beside his mistress and clearing a path for her through the city crowd. Then at their destination, he gently removes the sandals from her feet. In the elegy's concluding passage, however, even the solution which occasioned this second set of graceful and unhurried movements is rejected, and the poet is left to imagine yet another agitated movement, the pacing of Delia's next lover back and forth before her door.

But it is not the motion of the top or the procuress or the pacing lover that brings the poem to its close. The poem ends instead with the slow, relentless and recurring motion of water, which recalls its central image: Thetis/Delia bobbing slowly on the waves forever beyond the poet's reach. And so it appears that the real roots of his elegy's pessimism lie not in the wild movements of the poet's passion and despair but rather in the regular, almost gentle movement and change which characterize human affairs. The things we cherish most in life slip slowly away from us and this is, the poet tells us, the most frightening motion of all.

In human affairs the agent of this kind of motion is, of course, time, and so, quite understandably the poet again makes use of time and tense change as a structuring device. In this elegy the arrangement of tenses is both elegant and clear. The poem begins with two past-present- future sequences, then moves to two past-present sequences and finishes with three present-future sequences. Consider this further. In the opening lines the poet reflects upon his *past* boasting about being able to live

without Delia, recognizes his *present* anguish and condemns himself to
future chastisement. He then returns to the *past*, Delia's illness and his
care of her and then focuses on her *present* ingratitude, reflecting finally
on the idyllic *future* he had imagined for both of them. The first
sequence reflects the poet's understanding of life's rhythms: folly
followed by anguish and finally suffering. The second is similar but
makes folly the final or future term, for in it, service is followed by
ingratitude and ultimately by the evanescence of foolishly imagined bliss.
    The next two past-present sequences are brief. The poet imagines that
he had actually achieved bliss in the *past* but finds that those joys have
now fled. In the *past* he tried to forget Delia with wine and other
women, but her image, like that of Thetis haunts him *now*. The past
recedes as the elegy draws to a close and so three present-future
sequences bring it to a conclusion. The procuress has ushered in the
present lover and she *will* suffer for it if the poet's curse is fulfilled.
This possibility raises in the poet the faint hope that there may be even
now some justice for the faithful lover, and so he dreams of returning in
the *future* to the city where he *will* become Delia's faithful escort. But,
no, this too is an illusion. His poetry *is* powerless and the *future* holds
only a seemingly endless series of lovers who will fall victim to Delia
and unending change in their turn. It is this last imagined *future* that
confirms the poet in his pessimistic view: nothing is permanent, least of
all love, everything moves as if on the surface of an undulating sea and
slips away.
    Time is not, however, the only factor in this process. There is an
inherent instability in the very things we think of as real. To underline
this shifting vision of the world the poet employs another of his favorite
devices: the placement of similar images in different contexts and in
different perspectives. Children, for example, appear twice in the poem.
In the first instance the child is a high-spirited boy whose top moves in
the same manner as the poet's volatile emotions, but in the second
instance the children appear as docile and loving young slaves who play
happily on Delia's lap. The first image suggests desire and passion, the
second fulfillment. What seems the same is in fact different. Two older
women appear in the elegy. The first, a witch, helps to cure Delia with
her chants, with holy meal and with offerings to Hecate, the goddess of
the crossroads. The second, the procuress, destroys the love of Delia and
the poet and is cursed. One old woman fosters mutual love, the other
base and destructive lust. In the same manner similar activities are

viewed in different ways in the poem. The meal served to Messalla is an imagined joy but the meal to be eaten by the cursed procuress is a horror. The use of magic to cure Delia is salutary, but the spell which Delia is accused of casting on the poet brings heartache and pain.

In sum, Tibullus' focus on kinds of movement, the shifting of tenses and time frames and the resonating but often contrasting imagery all contribute to the thematic structure of this complex elegy whose final message seems to be: things change constantly in time and place, heart and mind. Nothing endures, least of all love.

✦   ✦   ✦

1.6

Introduction

The poet continues to learn that the world of lovers is filled with inconstancy and grief, and this elegy presents his reaction to that deepening understanding. Delia is deceiving him with another lover just as she had formerly deceived her husband or rich patron with him. Deceit breeds deceit; this is the hard truth. The fair face of love is itself a deception, and in this deeply ironic elegy the poet reveals his anguish and disappointment as he continues his pathetic search for a remedy for his unrequited passion.

At first he assigns blame for his disappointment to the male god, Cupid and to other men, his old rival as well as the new rivals who now seek Delia's favors. He explores the basic premise that Love is a deceitful prankster by recalling first his own instruction of Delia in the arts of deceit and then his old rival's gullibility and naiveté. The immediate problem, however, lies with Delia's new suitors. Their deceptions must be exposed and prevented and, to accomplish this, he now proposes an outlandish alliance. He imagines himself confessing, even boasting to his principal rival about his earlier seduction of Delia. Presenting this seduction as his credential, he then applies for a position as Delia's new guardian. Make me her protector, he proposes, and I will keep the crowd of young suitors away. I will follow her even to the temple of the women's goddess, the Bona Dea, whose festival, it appears, Delia took advantage of for meeting new admirers. The poet boasts that he will undergo any pain to protect Delia, boasts that he will remain unharmed, not suffering the blindness that was said to afflict men who illicitly viewed the Bona Dea's rites. Finally he predicts that, as an

51

old hand at lovers' tricks, he is bound to succeed in keeping Delia's new lovers away.

In the course of this fantasy, the poet attempts to enhance its plausibility with divine authority. A god, he asserts, told him to take this course. The priestess of Bellona, the goddess of war often identified with the Asian goddess Ma, who was, significantly, served by a group of temple prostitutes, spoke to him in a frenzy and gave him dire warnings about the fate of those who dare touch a woman under the protection of Love. But what of the woman herself? What if she, what if Delia herself is false? The poet considers this possibility in the second half of the elegy and imagines still other remedies. He turns first to Delia's mother, who once aided him in deceiving his rival and who, we assume, is still the abettor of Delia's infidelities. In a deeply sarcastic passage he blesses the old woman and asks her to become a teacher of chastity and fidelity. In return he promises absolute fidelity himself and agrees to endure Delia's mistreatment of him even when it is wholly undeserved. He prays in fact for the power to control his temper even when Delia unjustly abuses him physically.

At the conclusion of the elegy, the poet appeals directly to Delia, urging her to return his love freely rather than from a fear of punishment. In this voluntary fidelity, however, the poet has, it seems, little confidence, for he has deduced from the rules of love he has so painfully learned that constancy cannot be hoped for in the world of lovers. His only satisfaction lies in fact in the inevitable punishment of the faithless lover, a punishment captured by the image of Venus, who, as the elegy closes, is seen chastising an aging and faithless beauty who must now work upon a rented loom, mocked by throngs of young men who demand a cruel price for her youthful inconstancy.

Illogically and pathetically the poet closes with a couplet in which he prays that he and Delia may grow old together, examples of enduring love. We grasp the irony; if he is in earnest he is deceived yet once again. This final vision is yet another fantasy and a confirmation of the very gullibility to which he confessed at the beginning of the poem. The final couplet's consummation inscribes the poet's deepest longing but sadly contradicts the conclusion which the elegy's assumptions and premises logically demand.

Translation

Love, always, just to lead me on, you turn
A smiling face, then later, as I agonize,
Turn truculent and grim.
Why savage me?
Do gods themselves make boasts 5
While laying snares for men?
Well then, the nets are stretched for me.
Now Delia, clever bitch,
Is fondling god-knows-whom,
A love thief in the still of night. 10

O, she denies it time and time again.
Hard to believe! It's just the way
She keeps denying to her man
That she knew me, yes, me. Poor fool!
I taught her how to give the guards the slip, 15
To feign some cause for sleeping by herself,
To close the door without a hinge's creak.
My cleverness comes home to roost.
There was a time I gave her juice from herbs
To wipe away the bruise a passion-mate 20
Can cause by sinking teeth in lover's flesh.
But you, my fakir's foolish mate in bed,
Keep eyes on me as well
If you would keep the girl from going wrong.
Don't let her chatter with that swinging set 25
Or languish on some couch,
Her breasts on view above a plunging gown.
Take care she doesn't fool you with a nod
Or dip her finger in the wine and write
Upon the circle of a table top. 30
She's always on the town? The time to fear!
Even if she claims it's Bona Dea's rites,
To which we men may not draw near.

But no, just put her in my care.
Alone I'll follow her to shrines. 35

No need to fear the curse
Upon offending eyes of mine.
Often, I recall, I used to touch
Her hand and give as my excuse
The eyeing of a jewel or ring; 40
And often I would prompt your drowsiness
With wine while I, to win her, downed
Pure water in a sober cup.
I didn't mean to hurt you then.
Forgive. I'm telling all. 45
Love gave commands. Who can, I ask,
Take sword against the gods?
I am the one -
I'm not ashamed to tell the truth -
The one your dog would threaten 50
With his barking all night long.

But then, what need have you
Of such a sweet young thing,
Unable now to hold the prize you have?
What good's the key that's in your door? 55
She throws her arms around you, yes,
But her sighs are for another love,
Who's gone, and so she makes believe
That all at once the migraine's come again.
But here's the plan: just put her in *my* care, 60
And I will flee no savage whip
And never pull the shackles from my feet.
You pretty boys with fancy hair
Whose ample gowns flow billowing in the breeze,
Now keep your distance please. Let those who want 65
No guilt to follow meeting us by chance
Keep well away, keep well a block away.
It's what the god himself commands;
It's what the mighty priestess told,
Who spoke to me the truth 70
And sounded god herself,
For when Bellona's spirit stirs her up,
Berserk, she loses fear of biting flame

And coiled lash, but in a violent fit
She'll slash her arms with a double-bladed axe,   75
And, feeling nothing, bathe
The goddess' statue in the blood that bubbles up.
Side pricked by spear, with bloodied breast
With a knife fixed firmly in her side,
A gaping wound upon her breast,   80
She chants the things to come,
The things the mighty goddess prophesies.
"Be careful not to violate
The girl whom Love protects.
Just touch her and you'll feel regret in time   85
For the enormity of your offense;
Just touch her and your wealth
Will disappear like blood from these, my wounds,
Like ashes here the winds drive off.

Some punishment, sweet Delia, she foretold   90
For you as well; but if you'll just admit...
I'll pray that it be mild.
Nor is it just for you that I relent;
Your mother sways my mind,
That golden lady overcomes my wrath,   95
The one who brings you to me in the dark,
Who, filled with fear, in silence and in stealth,
Links groping lovers' hands,
Awaits me at the door at night
And from a distance knows   100
My footsteps as I come.
Live long, sweet lady. I'd give you
All the years that I myself deserve
If only god and nature would agree.
I'll love you, love that child of yours   105
Because of you, however she behaves.
Your blood is in her veins.
Just teach her to be chaste,
Although no ribbon holds her hair in place,
No matron's gown enfolds her feet.   110
And let the rules be hard for me as well -

Unable to admire another girl
Without her flying at my eyes
With sharpened nails, and if she thinks
I've gone astray, dragged by the hair,   115
Quite innocent, let me be thrown
Headlong into the street.
I would not lay a hand on you,
But if that madness ever seized my mind,
I'd pray they cut my hands away.   120
But, Delia, don't be chaste for fear
Of savagery. Be chaste instead
Because your mind and heart are true.
May given love, love taken too
Preserve you mine when I am gone.   125
For she who keeps no faith with men,
Undone by age, no money in her purse,
Pulls threads from spools with a trembling hand
And ties the leashes to a rented loom,
And as she washes strands she draws   130
From snowy fleece, a gang of rowdy boys
Looks on in wild delight, remarking how
The hag has reaped the misery she deserves.
And Venus on Olympus sees
Her weeping too and teaches us   135
How bitter she can be to those who are untrue.

O Delia, let these curses fall
On other girls; and let us, you and I,
Be models of true love, the two of us,
With silvered hair in years to come.   140

Commentary

As we have seen, this elegy is yet another lover's lament which
contains an account of the poet's deepening anguish and his hitherto
unsuccessful search for remedies. His search now leads him to imagine
quite fantastic and ironic solutions: an alliance with the very man he has
deceived and adulation of Delia's mother, who appears here as a
conspirator in Delia's infidelities. All of this is capped by a vision of

unending matrimonial bliss, which even the poet must realize is the most unlikely outcome of his present passion. Such is the elegy's primary message. What deeper significance does its text reveal? I would suggest that if we examine its imagery and structure more carefully, we will find that the poem is also a study of the relation of gods to humans, of men to women and of youth to age.

Consider first the manner in which motifs that treat the relations between the sexes and age groups are subtly interwoven. Three women appear: Delia who is young, her mother, who is old but not too old to abet lively intrigues, and the old hag who is pictured sitting at her loom tormented by young men who no longer find her attractive. Correspondingly, three men or groups of men also appear: the old rival, possibly a husband, who although not very old, is at least too old to deserve and satisfy Delia, the poet himself, a mature lover, and young men who appear several times: as Delia's new suitors, as the butt of the poet's rage and as the tormentors of the once haughty but now abandoned old hag at the loom. The poet's treatment of these figures presents a kind of calculus of age and sexuality. Youth is destined to attract and pursue youth and to deceive and ridicule age; while those in their middle years must either struggle in vain to prevent the success of youth's conspiracy against them as the poet does here, or like Delia's mother become the ally of youth. One thing, however, is quite clear in this intergenerational sexual reckoning: advanced age in both men and women is condemned to suffering and ridicule. The poet's final fleeting vision of the happy white-haired couple is unconvincing.

As the poet's exploration of these motifs proceeds, the gods make four appearances. Love or Cupid is introduced at once as the impish instigator of passion. He is drawn as a cruel dissembler who drives unfortunate lovers to their cruel fates, who forces them to love in spite of themselves. Two minor female goddesses then appear, the Bona Dea or women's goddess, who allows her rites to be used to mask the infidelities of Delia and, one imagines, other women, and Bellona, the goddess of war, whose ecstatic priestess warns, in a bloody scene of self-immolation, that vengeance will be wreaked on those who interfere with the true course of love. Finally at the very end of the elegy, Venus herself, Cupid's mother, makes a chilling appearance, displaying the forsaken hag as an example of how a life of passion and infidelity draws to a close. This final image presents the true conclusion of the poet's syllogism of love: that men and women, young and old, are the playthings of capricious and often malevolent divinities. The gods engender passion through deceit, abet and sanction it, and then, using the cruel contradictions of age, bring all to naught, punishing lovers for their own sport. It is not a heart-warming vision.

And so, beneath the surface of this elegy which seems yet another poet's lament and nothing more, there lies another structure which reveals a vision of the gods' manipulation of men and women at the various stages of their lives. In this scheme the order in which the various images appear is significant. The elegy begins with the instigator, Cupid, shifts at once to Delia's flirtations with young men, all of them abetted by the Bona Dea whose temple she uses as a trysting place, and then explores in a fanciful and ironic manner, the relationship between the mature poet and his aging rival, as well as the relation of both to the ever-threatening young.

At the very center of the elegy the most striking vision occurs. The priestess of Bellona, the war goddess, cries out in ecstacy, predicting the destruction of all those who interfere with the course of true love. Her appearance underlines the contradictions which the divinities' roles imply and is a frightening reminder as well of the connections between passion and aggression, love and war.

The following images are of age assisting youthful passion, and the poet draws a brief hope from these. But that hope too is short-lived. He recognizes, in an aside, that his own passion may itself be inconstant, imagines his future squabbles with Delia and presents us with a chilling tableau of the super-annuated coquette, poor, ugly and ridiculed. And behind this tableau stands Venus herself, the goddess of love who displays it as her handiwork.

It is possible that Tibullus had seen lovers like those alluded to in his final lines, lovers who had remained faithful to one another even unto old age. But in this elegy, as in most of his love poems, this possibility remains an unrealistic hope. The Venus he knew was a more terrifying deity. There is humor and sarcasm in the elegy, to be sure, but it is a very dark humor indeed. The careful reader will discern, I think, that the poet's comic and sarcastic fantasies are in fact pathetic and that the principal emotional power of this poem derives from the painful tension between the logic of its discourse of love and the fantastical projections of the doomed poet's longings.

✦   ✦   ✦

1.7

Introduction

The poet has been called upon to deliver a rather complicated congratulatory speech. The occasion is the celebration of both the triumph and birthday of his patron Messalla Corvinus. In fulfilling this request he borrows from three sub-genres and composes an elegy that is at once a song of triumph and praise for a conquering hero, a hymn honoring the Egyptian god Osiris, seen here as the god of civilization, and finally, a birthday song addressed to Messalla, his Birthday Spirit and his Genius.

On the surface this elegy, like many occasional pieces and the speeches they often mimic, seems to lack a carefully designed structure. It rambles on, one section connected to the next by seemingly chance associations of images and ideas. Here, as in other poems, however, Tibullus is employing an imagined setting to achieve verisimilitude as well as an impression, but only an impression, of randomness and spontaneity. As we shall see, the text concerns itself with more than its lyrical frame suggests at first reading.

The poet begins by focusing upon Messalla's triumph, which took place in September of 27 B.C. and upon the recent victories in Aquitania which it celebrated. In fact, Tibullus himself had accompanied his patron on this campaign and boasts in the poem about his part in it - a striking contrast to the poet's *persona* in other elegies. After attributing the victory of Messalla to Fate, the poet paints a picture of the general's triumph which includes a catalogue of the places which he and Messalla visited. These lie in or near Aquitania, the Roman province which

59

stretched from the Bay of Biscay along the Pyrenees to the Garonne River. The majority of the place names given belong in fact to rivers: the Garonne itself, the Atax or Aude, which flows into the Mediterranean at Narbonne, the Arar or Saone, which joins the Rhone at Lyon and the Liger or Loire. Several other places and people are alluded to as well: Tarbella Pyrene, the modern Tarbes, the Oceanus Santonici, the sea at the mouth of the Garonne, near which a tribe named the Santones lived, and finally the Carnuti, who were the inhabitants of the present-day Chartres.

At this point in the elegy the first apparently random shift of subject occurs. The names of these western places and people suggest in turn their counterparts, eastern sites which Messalla had also visited. The poet catalogues these as well, moving eastward from the Cydnus, a river in Cilicia in Asia Minor, to Taurus, a mountain identified with the present-day Bulgar Dagh, and on to Palestine and the city of Tyre, to which he attributes mankind's first attempts at seafaring. Continuing around the eastern end of the Mediterranean, he comes at last to the Nile, whose waters, he notes, playing upon a well known *topos*, irrigate the land parched by Sirius, the Dog star, and whose springs are unknown to men.

Here the poet seems to digress again. The Nile brings to mind the Egyptian god Osiris, the god of fertility and civilization, who in the cult of his sister and spouse Isis was annually slain and reincarnated in the form of a bull, and whose shrine at Memphis resounded each year with lamentation for that animal's death. The poet praises the god's civilizing powers and achievements, linking him with the Roman god Bacchus and inviting him at last to join the celebration that is underway.

This return to the present occasion with his invitation to the god Osiris is itself ingenious, but cleverer still is the way the poet moves his readers from a vision of the greater ceremony, the triumph, to the subsequent and more intimate birthday celebration. Here, as family and friends gather, Messalla's Genius, the spirit which both defines and protects him, is being honored. The customary offering to it, the cakes and Mopsopian honey from far-off Attica in Greece, are made, prayers are offered for the hero's offspring and a tribute is paid to his recent domestic achievement, the rebuilding of a section of the Via Latina, the great road that stretched south of Rome to Tusculum, Alba Longa and beyond. These rituals performed, the poet closes with the customary birthday wish: that the Birthday Spirit may return year after year, brighter and brighter with each return.

Translation

> This is the day the Fates foretold,
> The Fates, who spin the threads of doom
> Which no god can unbind.
> This is the day they said would have the power
> To scatter Aquitanians on the ground   5
> And make the River Atax shudder,
> Victim of the brave.
> These things have come to pass.
> Our Roman men have seen new triumphs come,
> And captive generals marched   10
> With arms bound fast, as you,
> Messalla, victor's laurel on your head,
> A car of ivory bore behind a dazzling team.
>
> Not without me these honors grew.
> Tarbes' Pyrenees are witnesses,   15
> Santonge's ocean shore.
> The Soane is witness, fleeting Rhone,
> The broad Garonne, blue-crystal streams of Loire
> That flow by Chartres' golden men.
>
> Or should I, Cydnus, make my song of you,   20
> Who gently bends your placid stream
> In silent rivulets, above its shoals,
> A glass of blue; or tell how tall
> Cold Taurus stands that brushes clouds
> With a sky-blown peak and feeds Cilicia's men?   25
> Why sing the white and holy dove
> That flies unharmed among the teeming towns
> Of Palestine or make my tale of Tyre,
> The first to trust its freighters to the wind
> And scan from towers the vastness of the sea?   30
> Why tell of how the fertile Nile,
> When desert winds split Egypt's mud-caked fields,
> Swells great with summer flood?

O Father Nile, how can I give the reason why
Or name the place in which you hide your head?   35
Because of you the land requires no rain.
Dry grass need send no prayers to stormy Jove,
And rustic folk sing hymns to you
And gaze in awe as if on their Osiris,
Catechized to weep for Memphis' holy bull.   40
Osiris was the first to build
A plough with craftsman's hands,
The first to stir the soft rich soil with steel,
The first to give his seeds to untried land
And gather fruit from trees that were unknown.   45
He taught the tender vine to wed the stake
He taught green leaves to fall
Beneath cruel pruning hooks. To him
In season grapes first gave sweet vintages
Pressed beneath a simple farmer's feet: 50
The drink that taught us how to bend
Our voices in a song and move
Our unschooled limbs in measured beats.
Just so lord Bacchus brings the farmer's heart
That's wasted by unending toil   55
Release from gloom and woe.
And Bacchus brings repose to men enslaved
In spite of ankles' metal clang
And shackle's bite that never yields.
No grief, no gloomy cares are yours,   60
Osiris, no, but dance and song
And love as light and free as you,
And multi-colored flowers, ivied brows
And yellow gowns that fall around a maiden's feet,
And purple robes and flute's sweet song   65
And wicker basket schooled
In all the secrets of your holy rites.

Come here to celebrate with us
His Genius in our games,
His Genius in our dance.   70
Drown temples now in endless cups of wine.

why this strong

Let scented ointments hang in drops
Upon his bright and shining hair
And let him carry garlands fresh
On head and neck. *Today's* god, come,   75
And let me give an incense offering
And bring you cakes made sweet
With honey from Mopsopius' land.
And may your children grow to build
Upon their father's work and stand   80
With honor 'round you in your age.
And when the tourists linger there in Tusculum
In brilliant Alba with its antique shrine,
Let them note your monumental road.
Your wealth it was that laid the gravel base,   85
That saw the flint rocks fitted, edge to edge.
And farmers too had better bless your name,
Late nights, when back from town,
They make their way without a fall.

You, Birthday Spirit, years to come,   90
Come brighter, brighter still,
To take our celebration here.

Commentary

Beneath the celebratory frame of this elegy there lies a message that is significantly broader and deeper. At this deeper level the poem deals with the natural world of time and space, with human movement and civilizing initiatives and with the relationship of these to the supernatural order, both Fate and the gods. It is this message that explains the poem's dramatic shifts in time and place and its fascination with movement both natural and human, images of which constitute a thematic focus in the text.

The elegy begins with a reference to "this day,' the *present*, which is immediately explained as a fulfillment of what was ordained in the remote past by the *Parcae* or Fates. Thus in these opening lines, the poet presents his readers with a world in which gods and men are crucial actors, but actors in a drama that is preordained. In short, he gives us a three-tiered world in which gods and men act to shape the time and space of the natural world in the manner destiny requires.

Within this conceptual frame the remote past of the Fates gives way in the text to the recent past and Messalla's campaign in the West. In fact, this part of the poem links the recent past in Gaul with the present in Rome, where the hero's triumph took place, and in both places the theme of movement is at once highlighted by a series of images of motion, the motion of nature as seen in the vital flow of rivers and the motion of human beings, both fettered and free, that we observe as the armies, the captive commanders and the hero himself move through scenes of conquest and triumph. It quickly becomes clear that the theme of motion is linked to the elegy's patriotic tone. These images also tell us that Rome is "on the move" in triumphal processions, in conquests and in the achievements of the national destiny that will follow. Those barbarous western lands, just won for her will be the object of Rome's civilizing thrust, and so Messalla's triumph looks two ways in time: to the past foundations of civilization and to Rome's future cultivation of the newly won western lands.

The sudden shift in focus from West to East is not therefore unprepared for. The poet now turns our attention to the times and places in which civilization finds its roots: in the ancient East. And the theme of movement continues. Now, however, the movements of nature are modified by the innovative movements of human beings. The sea has its own motion but the Tyrians use it to sail upon. The Nile fertilizes its banks but farmers take advantage of its motion to initiate their own agricultural endeavors. Thus, in this part of the elegy we find that we have ourselves been moved imagistically in both time and space to the predestined origins of civilization in which both nature and humanity played their parts. Nor are the gods absent. We are quickly reminded of the role played by Osiris, the counterpart of Dionysus/Bacchus, the civilizer and, significantly, *triumphator*, who introduces not just agriculture and viticulture but the arts as well. These in turn give rise to yet other human movements: the crushing of grapes yes, but also the tripping of carefree feet in the dance, even, we are reminded, the lightened tread of the fettered slave.

Has the poet, we wonder, forgotten Messalla, as he dwells upon the civilizing god's accomplishments? Not at all. If the destiny preordained by fate is to be achieved, then the human actors must play their role as well, and so we are cleverly moved once again back to Rome, where the far more intimate and personal birthday party is underway. Even the supernatural order will be personalized here. The Genius of Messalla, the counterpart in his individual life to the Fates, is presented, and all of the ritual obligations to that very personal spirit are carried out. As the poem draws to a close our attention is drawn to a future that is both personal and marked by civilized tranquility. It will be peopled by Messalla's grandchildren and punctuated by birthday parties to come. Finally, Romans themselves will recall Messalla not for military conquests alone but for his works of peace, among them his rebuilding of the Via Latina, along which both sightseers and farmers may move in security. Movement again, here at the conclusion, not the movement of soldiers or captive general as at the outset, but the casual movement of those enjoying civilization and its benefits. This final prayer, which the poet sees himself delivering at the party, emphasizes that Messalla's military achievements which his triumph celebrated are matched by cultural achievements that the birthday celebrants must recognize as part of the destiny referred to as the elegy began.

✦ ✦ ✦

1.8

Introduction

In this elegy the poet once again presents himself as a teacher or counselor in the affairs of the heart, beginning by emphasizing his own romantic experience and the knowledge of love it has given him.   He has been observing a young couple in love and boasts that he has seen through their behavior at once, not because he possesses any special powers of divination but because he himself has suffered as they are suffering.

The poet then addresses one of the lovers, leaving it unclear whether it is a boy or a girl to whom he is speaking. Indeed, he deliberately plays with his readers by harping upon a vanity and fastidiousness of dress that suggest the behavior of a young woman, only to reveal a few lines later that it is a young man he is addressing, a young man who is apparently something of a dandy. In spite of his own vanity, however, this boy is ravished by his mistress' beauty no matter how casual she is about her own appearance. Why is this the case? Not, the poet insists because of magic. Magic may charm crops out of a neighbor's field, may charm snakes, would even bring the moon down out of the sky, did people not take care to bang on pots and pans to prevent its descent, but love needs no magic to work its ends. A mere kiss, the touch of a thigh is enough to kindle the flames of passion.

The poet now addresses the girl, who appears to be present before him, but who, like the boy, is left nameless at this point. His lecture to her contains echoes of his own complaints to Delia. He warns against older lovers who bring expensive gifts and extols youth and its performance in the camp of love. Finally he warns the girl to take advantage of youth while it lasts, driving home this warning by painting a vivid image of old age and of the pathetic efforts of an aging lovely to keep her beauty alive.

Then, quite suddenly, the poet turns his attention back to the boy and refers to him by name. He is in fact Marathus, the youth whom he himself had pursued in the past, whose favors he presumably enjoyed, whose secrets he shared. With the speaking of this name a new range of semantic possibilities opens up, new levels of meaning spring into being. The lovers are not just any lovers The boy is the poet's own former favorite. New opportunities for irony now exist in the text and the theme of a possible bittersweet revenge makes an appearance.

The poet now proceeds to intercede even more fervently on Marathus' behalf. He even mimics him, placing on his lips a long and ironic speech of complaint in which the boy's daring and skill as a lover and novice teacher of love are stressed, but in which as well the hard heart of his beloved - not unlike his own hard heart and its earlier rejection of the poet himself - renders all of these qualities ineffective. A reader familiar with Tibullus' elegies recognizes these themes at once. The poet has, it seems, brought all of his poetic artillery to bear on behalf of his former favorite, enjoying, we suspect, laments not unlike those which the boy himself may have ridiculed in the past when he was Delia's rival.

And now the poet names the girl. Her name is Pholoe, and she is clearly a stubborn and heartless Pholoe. She will not give in to Marathus, and her obstinacy gives the poet the opportunity not only to warn her about the vengeance the gods will take on her in the future but to tell as well the tale of how arrogant and heartless Marathus himself was when, as a boy, he was being pursued by male lovers. The tables have been turned. The old lover now enjoys a bittersweet revenge but finds himself still sufficiently under the boy's spell to sympathize with him nevertheless. And so he tries one last time to persuade the girl to yield by using an argument that he employed, we recall, in the past: the beloved who refuses to listen to a true lover's plea will suffer in time and long to relive the past whose opportunities she failed to grasp.

Translation

> Impossible to keep me in the dark
> About what lovers' nods, the sound

Of soft and wheedling words are all about.
No fortune teller's pick-up-sticks,
No livers that divine the divine,   5
No bird's song need foretell for me
How this will end. Venus herself, with whip
Has drilled me many times, my arms bound tight
By that fair lady's magic knot.
So drop dissimulation, please;   10
The goddess puts a crueller flame
To those she sees refuse to stretch
Their limbs upon her bed.

What good is all that now:
The times you brushed your silky hair.   15
Those endless combings, this way, that?
What good's the painting of your cheeks
With blushing rouge? What good's the fingernails
Pared with a manicurist's touch?
All for nothing now the clothes,   20
For nothing all the change of robes,
Those dainty boots that clutch
Your ankle with their buckle tight.
She can drive you mad,
No make-up on her face at all,   25
Just tieing up her radiant hair with casual grace.
Some hag, I should suppose,
Has hexed you in the stillest hour of night;
With spells she got you, got you, yes,
With color-draining herbs. A charm, I know,   30
Once brought the crops out of a neighbor's field.
A charm can force an angry snake
To stay its slippery coils. A charm will try
To bring the moon down from her car,
Would do it too, if people didn't raise   35
The sound of clanging pots and pans.
But why this fuss about a hurt
Inflicted on a boy by spells, by herbs?
Beauty needs no help from magic tricks.
The ill begins when bodies touch,   40

When, after lingering kisses, then -
A woman's thigh begins to press a man's.

So you, sweet girl, remember well
To be less grudging with the boy,
For Venus visits punishment   45
On mean and joyless work like that.
Don't ask for gifts. Let white-haired wooers give
To warm their chilly members
On the pillow of your lap.
A young man is a dearer thing than gold.   50
His smooth bronze face aglow,
No scratchy beard to chaff your love's embrace.
Just let your gleaming arms lie languishing
Beneath his neck, and say to hell
With royal wealth. He's shy perhaps?   55
Well, even Venus found the way
To sleep in secret with a timid boy,
Press tender breast to breast,
And give a panting lover
Wet kisses sliced by jabbing tongues,   60
To fix upon her lover's neck
Notations of her bite.

No gems, no stones bring joy to her
Who, shivering, sleeps alone,
Desired by not a single man;   65
And O, too late love is recalled,
And too late youth, when white old age
Has stained a head that's bent with years.
They study beauty then. Then hair is changed
And dyed with rinds of ripened nuts   70
To mask the years. They take care then
To pull white hairs out by the root,
To pull their skin away and make
A youthful face return. But you, my dear,
While in the flowered springtime of your years,   75
Consume its joys, for springtimes pass,
And pass on feet that never limp.

No torture for Marathus, girl.
What glory in a beaten boy? Turn heart that's hard,
My flower child, to wiser, older loves;   80
But spare, I beg you, this young man.

His illness is not grave.
A little pale from too much love.
How often, after all, the love-sick boy
Hurls sad complaints against an absent love,   85
'Til all the world stands drenched with tears.
"You turn me down," he cries. "And why?
I might have bribed the guard.
God himself legitimizes love's deceit.
All Venus' darker tricks are known to me: 90
The drawing of a shallow breath,
The stealing of a silent kiss,
The power to creep the midnight streets,
To unbolt doors in silence and in stealth
Wherever you may choose.   95
What good to me is all this skill,
When this cruel love-child spurns her sorry love
And flees his bed? And even when she's sworn,
She's sudden-faithless, plays me false.
Then all night long, with agonies in troops,   100
It's mine to lie awake,
Imagining that she will come,
Believing that whatever moves
The footfall must be hers."

Stop crying, son; you will not break her will.   105
Your eyes grow red and swollen with your tears.
But Pholoe, take my warning too:
The gods dislike stand-offish girls,
And no amount of incense at their fanes
Will expiate your guilt.   110
This same Marathus made this once his sport,
Deceiving love-sick boys, not knowing then
A vengeful god sat silent just behind
His head. And often, so they say, he mocked

Unhappy lovers' tears, detained   115
A yearning caller with some feigned delay.
Now *he* hates haughtiness. Now *he*
Is all displeasure if the bolt upon
Some heavy door stands squarely in his way.

To you as well a punishment will come,   120
Unless you call a halt to pride; and then,
Then in the prayers you make desire will stir
To summon back this very day.

Commentary

This elegy is both playful and poignant. Its structure is determined by
its playfulness and that structure produces in turn its poignancy, a
poignancy generated by the poem's subtle and indirect handling of the
passage of time and by the displacement and alteration of love which that
passage brings about. Knowledge and lack of knowledge of this sad
process provide the catalyst for the playful interaction between the poet
and the two young lovers, but knowing and not knowing is important in
yet another way. The poet cleverly withholds knowledge from us, his
readers, sharing information about both identities and attitudes slowly
and in a manner that guides our own emotional response to the text and
produces at its conclusion its lyrical catharsis.

The elegy begins with a statement by the poet that he is
knowledgeable, even expert at love and cannot be deceived about the
actions of lovers. What is more, he stresses that this knowledge of his
is genuine because it has been gained through experience and suffering.
We are alerted at once to the fact that the poem will have a bittersweet
quality; it will deal with young love but that love will be seen through
the eyes of an experienced lover. This lens will inevitably give the
presentation of the present love affair a somewhat ironic and even
pathetic quality. The elegy is structured in such a way, however, that
the depth of that irony is not revealed to the reader at once.

Two devices, one thematic, one semantic, will give this poem its
shape: the contrasting of the poet's knowledge of the true nature of love
with the ignorance and deception of the young lovers and the clever
withholding of information from the reader. The first device is shaped
largely through the use of powerful imagery which distinguishes between

reality and illusion, true meaning and false. The carefully juxtaposed images fall into several easily recognizable categories. Sensuous and sexual images which represent reality and true meaning are opposed to cosmetic images and images of dress which represent illusion and false meaning. In the same manner, images of magic and dark ritual are opposed to images of erotic pursuit and desire. Finally, images of youth and its natural beauty are opposed to age and its ugliness, its remorse and its vain attempts at recapturing youth. As the poet instructs his two young pupils in this seminar on love, he weaves for them and for us a rich poetic tapestry which presents visually both the world's false notions about love and his own wisdom.

This graphic and imagistic structure is complemented by a linear one which controls, as the poem moves forward, the reader's understanding of the dramatic situation. By the time we reach the elegy's conclusion, this second linear structure will have assimilated the first and its messages into itself, and using it, will produce the emotional charge the poem carries. To understand this, we need to review the stages in which the poet moves his reader from ignorance to awareness.

At the outset, the reader knows only that the poet is addressing someone in love. There is no suggestion that more than one person is present and no names are given. Then, with the treatment of the lover's primping we are given the false impression that the individual being addressed is a girl. But this is a false start, the poet's first little joke, for when he points out that: "*She* can drive you mad, no make-up on her face at all," we are forced to conclude that the listener is in fact a boy. Next, the poet turns and says, "So you, sweet girl, remember well to be less grudging with the boy." The girl is present as well, it seems, and the emotional field of the elegy is dramatically more complex than we had imagined. The greatest surprise comes, however, with the naming of the boy more than halfway through the poem: "No torture for Marathus, girl." Marathus, we know from an earlier elegy, was the poet's own beloved, his *puer delicatus* or "toy boy." Now the emotional field is given, as we noted in the introduction to this elegy, a whole new level, a new circuitry that will guide the emotions of the three principals in the love seminar and guide our emotional responses as well.

The reader must raise at this point the question of the poet's attitude toward his former favorite. Will he use his superior knowledge of affairs of the heart to take revenge, perhaps to mock the boy? There have already been signs at the outset that this may occur. The temptation to take revenge must certainly be great, and yet he once loved the boy, perhaps loves him still.

Not long before the end of the poem and just as the poet reveals how he will in fact treat his former love, the girl herself is named. Why? Her name, Pholoe, is derived from one of two Greek place names and may suggest mountain remoteness, a not inappropriate association given her own haughty stand-offishness. It is more likely, however, that her naming here is meant first to personalize the dramatic situation whose final resolution we are about to witness, and second to remind us of the poet's playfulness throughout the poem. It is as if he were saying to us, "You see how cleverly I have manipulated your emotions by keeping you in the dark. Here, if it interests you, is the girl's name too."

In any case our knowledge of the situation is now complete and we can turn our full attention to what the poet feels and what he will do. What do we find? He is not able to forget and forgive entirely and gives in to the temptation to taunt Marathus by reminding him of his own youthful arrogance and by highlighting the irony implicit in his present anguish. Nor, on the other hand, has the power of his love for the boy faded entirely, and so he uses his own superior knowledge of love to make one last attempt to soften Pholoe's heart. Here the graphically treated theme of truth and falsity is united with the linear treatment of ignorance and awareness. Does the poet's final plea on behalf Marathus spring from the realization that the boy's suffering in love parallels his own? More important, does it provide a true understanding of love or is it too delusionary? If it is delusionary, by what motives is it driven? To that question we must provide a response ourselves, for as we come to the end of the elegy, we find ourselves in an emotional field that is not only complex and ironic but ambiguous as well. The lyric catharsis of the poem must embrace that ambiguity, and indeed may find its very ground in it.

1.9

Introduction

The poet has discovered that his favorite, Marathus, is having an affair with another man. The rival is old and ugly (Could he be the ugly husband of Pholoe in the preceding elegy, or, even more interesting, the husband of Delia?) but also rich and powerful, and it is with his wealth that he has stolen the boy away. Angry and jealous, the poet launches a bitter attack on both the boy and his new lover in a rambling lament more remarkable for its sarcasm and bile than for its rationality. Deeply hurt by Marathus' infidelity, he begins with the curious declaration that he does not in fact really care about the boy's deceit. But, he warns, the gods will certainly care and will send Marathus the punishment he deserves. Does the poet really want them to punish the boy? No, he retracts his threat at once. In fact, he then prays that Marathus be permitted to commit this one transgression with impunity. After all, he admits, the boy did it for profit and that, as everyone knows, is the way of the world.

Punishment, however, continues to prey upon the poet's mind. He now dwells upon other forms of punishment soon to come: on the disappearance of the rival's gifts and on the horrors of the journey which Marathus is even now planning to make with him.. Enjoying these prophecies of doom, the poet recalls his instruction of Marathus in the past and develops for his own pleasure as well as for the boy's edification the I-told-you-so theme. He had warned Marathus that this kind of prostitution would incur the wrath of Venus, and had warned him that it could not be hidden and that the gods often caused men's darkest secrets to be revealed in drunkenness and sleep.

The roots of the poet's grief are now set forth with greater clarity. He recalls the happy days of their mutual affection, his own doting upon Marathus and the boy's promises to be faithful no matter how lavish a rival's offer of gifts. Let them, he had said, offer him the rich lands of Campania and Falernia, renowned for their produce and wine, and still he would not prove false. And there is more to remember. The poet recalls how he himself had aided Marathus in his love affair with a girl, very probably, we surmise, the Pholoe of the preceding poem. In those days the poet acted as a go-between in hope of being himself rewarded with Marathus' love. Stupidly he trusted his beloved, even wrote poetry in praise of the boy. But now he is ashamed to write poetry and prays that either Vulcan, the god of fire, or some river's current carry off his poems and destroy them. With this wish, the theme of punishment, briefly become self-punishment, reenters the elegy.

There is, of course, someone else who must be punished, and so the poet now turns to the old rival and heaps curses on his head. He prays for the infidelity of the man's wife. Seizing the opportunity to heap scorn on the interloper's lecherous head, he compares the behavior of the man's promiscuous wife with the debauchery of his sister and then goes on to mock the rival's stupid obliviousness to his wife's flirtatious behavior. How can he imagine, the poet asks, that her seductive dress and manner are aimed at impressing him, a gouty old man, when in fact it is a younger lover she is trying to attract?

This vivid characterization of the disgusting rival reminds the poet of the inescapable and disgusting truth: Marathus now lavishes his favors upon this foul and stinking creature. The imagined vision of their kisses suggests to him a bestial liaison that cries out for punishment and revenge. And these will come, he exclaims, resuming the punishment theme, for when this present lover cools or is revealed for what he is, then Marathus will find the poet occupied with another love and able, now that he is freed from his servitude to the boy, to hang up an offering of thanksgiving for his deliverance in the temple of Venus.

Translation

> Why, if you were bent
> On spoiling our sad love,
> Did you keep giving promises,
> Only to break them on the sly?

Poor boy, a man can hide   5
His faithlessness at first,
But vengeance comes, soon or late
On silent feet.

Be easy on him, gods above.
Alright for lovely boys to injure gods   10
Just once and feel no punishment.
For profit farmers harness bulls and grasp their ploughs,
Pursue the muscled working of the land;
For profit constant stars lead rolling ships
Through waters that obey the wind.   15
With gifts this boy of mine was won.
May god turn all those gifts to ash,
To waters that are doomed to seep away;
And *he* will pay the punishment *I* set,
As dirt and hair all ruffled by the wind   20
Filch away his once good looks.
His face will burn, in scorching sun
His hair itself will burn as well.
Long walks will blister his uncallused feet.
How many times I warned him thus: 25
Do not pollute your beauty for mere gold,
For often horrors manifold
Lie hidden at the bottom of a purse.
To him who, money's captive,
Dares violate his love,   30
A harsh, soul-crushing Venus comes.

No, sooner singeing flame put to my head,
A sabre to my side, and sooner cut
My back with twisted whips. No hope
Of hiding stratagems of sin. God knows   35
And won't permit your treachery to hide.
The god has given silent slaves
The right, when they are deep in wine,
To speak their piece. The god himself
Bids men still fast asleep to utter words   40
And speak against their will

Of things that should remain unsaid.
All this I spoke and now I am ashamed
That, speaking, I did weep,
Threw myself before your tender feet.   45
Those days you used to swear
You'd never auction honor off,
No matter what the price,
For neither pounds of gold nor gems,
Not if Campania was the offer made,   50
Or Falernia, that lies in Bacchus' palm.
With words like those you might have snatched
The starlight from the sky, for all I knew,
Made currents stay their catapulting course.
You even wept, but I,   55
Untrained in treachery, like a trusting child
Kept wiping dry your moistened cheek.
What should I do... if you were not in love?
That girl! I pray she takes your lead
And plays the flirt. How many times late nights   60
I carried torches at your side,
So no one else would catch your words;
And often too, when you had lost all hope,
She came to you - my work - and hid
Behind the door with veiled head.   65
And then, poor man, I died the death,
While nurturing the foolish hope
That I was loved. I might have been
More wary of your snares but sang
Your praise instead, my wits gone wild.   70
And now I am ashamed of what we were,
The Muse and I and all that work-
I wish that Vulcan with his hungry flame
Would burn the verses up,
That clear and running streams would come   75
And blot the letters out for good.

But you, stand far away
Who scheme your beauty's sale and bring back home
In handfuls beauty's asking price;

And you who dared corrupt the boy   80
With all your gifts, I hope your wife,
Who cheats and cheats and never pays the price,
Laughs loud in bed at you,
Then lies beside you languishing,
Her nightgown buttoned tight,   85
When she's worn out her younger love
With service done in secret; and I hope
Another's trace is always in your bed,
And that your house lies open wide
To all who feel desire. I hope   90
They say your wife drinks more,
Retires greater troops of men than that slut,
Your sister does, for she, the rumor goes,
Will captain the carouse for Bacchus sake
Until the car of Lucifer
Rides to rouse the day;   95
And no one more than she has strength
To gorge herself upon the night,
Arranging the varieties
Of her wanton sensuality.
Your wife is carefully schooled, and you,   100
You stupid fool, do not catch on,
When she tries on new moves for you in bed.
Do you suppose she sets her hair for *you*
And combs those wispy curls with a fine-toothed comb,
Suppose your face is what persuades your wife   105
To wear those golden bracelets on her arms,
Step out, alluring, in a purple gown?
It's not for you, but for some boy
She wants to gaze upon her gorgeous form,
For whom she'd gladly down in doom   110
Your wealth, your house, and do it all,
No sinful spouse, but fleeing, girl
Of breeding that she is, your old man's arms,
Your foul and gouty corporeality.
To think this is the man my boy   115
Now lies beside in bed! If he'll do this,
I'd say he has the guts

To screw some filthy animal!

And did you dare to sell
Caresses once reserved for me,   120
Bring another, your mind unhinged,
The kisses that were mine?
The time will come for you to weep,
When another holds me in his power,
A haughty ruler in the place   125
Where you had ruled before.

Your punishment will bring me joy,
And I'll hang up a golden palm
To Venus who has earned my love;
And on it tell my tale: Tibullus,   130
Whom you rescued from a faithless love,
Hangs up this palm to you,
And, goddess, prays that you will turn
Your face in gratitude to him.

Commentary

Perhaps better than any poem in the collection this elegy provides the reader with a clear, even stark representation of Tibullus' vision of the dualistic universe in which human affairs are conducted. We are shown on the one hand the world of the grosser elements, of elemental passions and human infirmity and on the other the ethereal world of the stars and the gods, the immutable realm of true love to which human beings can only aspire and to which they must answer for their transgressions of its laws. It is important to emphasize at once that these realms provide not only a physical setting in which human actors perform but a cognitive and moral setting as well. The world of gross matter is also one in which deception and sin not only thrive but are virtually inevitable. It is a world in which the emotions are corrupted by the elements in their various forms: wine and gold, and by the basest of human drives: depraved sexual passion and greed. Opposite this world stands an etherial realm which breeds the nobler passions and loves, those which are both courtly and selfless, a realm which both measures and judges human behavior by its standards and inevitably sends punishment to those who fall short.

The present elegy charts the interaction of these two realms, using a set of lovers, the poet among them, as specimens of human behavior. Within the dramatic framework outlined above, this charting of love is achieved through the careful arrangement of themes and images. Tibullus' poetic strategy reveals itself at once for the poet begins by drawing a contrast between the two realms, between the gods by whom men swear and the fickleness of mankind's pathetic loves, between the perjury which characterizes human intercourse and the unfailing and inevitable punishment which the divine order inflicts.

The imagery of the lines that follow emphasizes this contrast further. The elemental appears in all of its forms: earth, water, wind and the ashes of a fire, and the immutable realm is represented by the stars whose reliability is contrasted with the erratic motion of ships tossed about by the winds and the sea. What is more, the poet links mutability and fickleness with the inevitable punishment which the finer realm will inflict. The gifts of rich lovers are seen as being dissolved into ash and water and the beloved's beauty is in time worn away.

As we are told more about the situation of the principals in this lyric drama the elegy becomes more personal. The poet turns to the past and recalls his own infatuation with Marathus and their promises to one another. Here too the same images and themes recur: the theme of deception, of the selling of insubstantial beauty for insubstantial wealth. Once again images of the grosser world, personalized in this context, proliferate: flowing tears, the flames of a lover's torches, the tongue-loosening wine, the farmland of Campania and Falernia. Nor does the poet allow us to lose sight of the immutable world. Not only are Venus and the Muses present but once again, the stars appear as well. Indeed they provide a striking example of how the two realms interact, for under the influence of Marathus' false oaths, the poet admits that he might well have imagined that the stars themselves had been dragged down from their places in the heavens, a striking image of the power of deception to destabilize the certainties of the immutable world to which human love aspires. But the frailty of all that lies below the stars has carried the day in the drama we are observing. The tears of lover and beloved blend as one prays for assurances and the other responds with emotional but insubstantial promises. It is a scenario which leads inevitably to the rejection of the higher realm by both of the principals. Marathus rejects Venus in his infidelity and the poet himself rejects the

Muses and the poetry they inspired.

As the poem moves to its conclusion, the baseness of the gross and mutable world is further explored. The poet's presumably noble love is contrasted with the behavior of not only the new rival but of his wife and sister as well. Here the darkness of the imagery effaces the nobler realm and its images fade for a time from view. Only the brief appearance of Lucifer, the morning star, which significantly unmasks the scenes of debauchery inscribed in these lines, relieves the poet's catalogue of human depravity. We glimpse a world otherwise in the clutches of gross matter, a world of drunkenness, promiscuity, foul disease and even bestiality, linked as before with images of deceit: the marks of his wife's lover in a man's bed, the wife's newly mastered sexual techniques and her frantic attempts to turn herself into an alluring seductress. The poet saves the strongest of this negative imagery for last, for we are given just before the poem's conclusion a picture of the rival lover, racked by the gout and smelling like an animal, embracing and kissing the poet's darling boy, who himself whispers to the old man the same sweet nothings which the poet himself had whispered to him.

Here is the pit of craven sensuality and the essence of lying treachery, the elemental realm at its worst. This is not quite the end of course. As Tibullus has reminded us several times, the world above looks down on human beings mired in the world of pure sensuality and deceit. Like Lucifer it sheds light on the sorry spectacle of human infidelity. And here too Venus sees and sends retribution. The poet will find a new love, we are told, and Marathus, forsaken by his rich lover, will weep for his loss. All true? Perhaps punishment will come, but what about Venus' kindness to the poet? Can that be counted on? We note as we finish the poem that the poet feels that both an offering and a prayer are in order. Perhaps complete justice is less certain than punishment even in the etherial world of the gods.

✦ ✦ ✦

1.10

Introduction

This elegy presents the reflections of a frightened man. The poet appears to be taking part in a military expedition. He has not yet reached the battlefield but sits alone in his quarters, conjuring up the images of warfare and longing for escape and peace. This frame is not made entirely clear, however, as the elegy begins. The opening lines suggest instead a rather detached and philosophical consideration of war, its origins, its effects, its causes and its opposite, peace. It is, in fact, only with the mention of peace that the poet reveals his own situation fully. As he longs for the life that existed in that simple golden age before greed bred violence and strife among men, he reveals that this desire is not hypothetical and does not spring from detached reflections alone. He is in fact on the way to a very real battle, and somewhere, he tells us, an enemy soldier is waiting with a sword that may yet find its way into his flesh.

This image terrifies him and, in his fear, he turns to prayer, addressing the Lares, his household gods. They protected him as a child, he recalls, and he begs that they protect him in the same way now. As this prayer unfolds, it becomes clear that these simple protective divinities and the world they foster are in fact linked by the poet to the simple golden age that existed before the advent of war. Unable to achieve a transition in time to that age, he longs now for a transition in space, a return home, where in a kind of private golden age he may take refuge in the religious rituals of his childhood years.

This poetic regression cannot, however, efface the images of war which his fear has evoked. He now imagines a battleworn veteran, boasting of his military achievements and drawing upon a tabletop the diagrams of his past campaigns. The vision of this lone heroic survivor conjures in turn, however, a larger and perhaps truer vision of the fruits of war: throngs of dead warriors wandering through the underworld. This, the poet recognizes, is really the significant outcome of war: the hastening of death, the opening up of a shorter road to human carnage. And if it is such, he hastens to add, it is for another man, not for him. He is in no haste to behold Cerberus, the monstrous dog that guards the gates of Hell, or to greet Charon, the ferryman who transports the dead across the river Styx to their final abode.

What *does* he want? Peace, of course and all of the things that accompany it: a long life, a happy marriage, crops and herds in abundance and, finally, to forget for a time even the cares that peace breeds, a little wine. He longs, in short, for a time in which the plough shines bright with use and the soldier's gear hangs unused, gathering rust in a remote storeroom.

It is perhaps the reference to wine that suggests in turn revelry and drunkenness, and these now bring to mind images of the sexual violence these activities can breed even in peacetime. The poet now imagines a drunken farmer attacking his wife, as Cupid, a bemused spectator, furnishes both with the crude eloquence their love bout requires. Even here, the poet reflects, as he pictures the scene, violence can become excessive. A drunken man may go beyond the permissible violence to garment and coiffure and inflict bodily harm on his love. Outrageous behavior, he exclaims. Such violence is, after all, too like the violence of warfare, and the man who engages in it should instead go off to battle with spear and shield in hand. His work is not the work of Venus.

The poet himself is, he tells us, far from such behavior in either love or war. And so he closes with a final prayer for the advent of peace, pictured here as a female goddess bearing the fruits of the earth, portrayed as she was in the iconography of the poet's day. This is the elegy's final vision, a vision which stands in stark contrast to the earlier view of the barren landscape of the Hell to which the dead are led.

Translation

> Who was it first produced a fearful sword?
> What kind of man? An animal he was
> And made of iron. Then slaughter came for men,
> Then battles had their birth. To grim death then
> They opened up a shorter road.   5

Perhaps the poor man shouldn't bear the blame;
The things he gave for use on savage beasts
We turned to ills our own:
A curse rich gold brought in. There were no wars
When beechwood cups were placed beside our food;   10
No citadel, no rampart then;
And rams, carefree, went off
To sleep among the dappled flocks.

Then I might have had a common life
And never known a soldier's sorry arms,   15
Nor heard with fluttering heart the trumpet's call,
But now I'm dragged to war, must face the fact
Some soldier on the other side
Bears arrows doomed to dangle in my flank.
O save me, Lares,   20
Who were protectors of my father's house,
Just as you nourished me, a child,
Who scampered at your feet.

No shame that you are carved from some old log.
You graced my father's house just so.   25
Men kept their word far better then,
When gods of wood stood humbly dressed
Within their tiny shrines,
Won over with an offering of wine,
With garland stalks of grain   30
Upon their hallowed heads.
The man whose prayer was granted then
Would bear himself the sacrificial cake,
And after him, his little girl,
Attending, brought the honey in a comb.   35
O Lares, you household gods,
Drive from my side the brazen tools of war;
*****
And I will make a country sacrifice
And kill a pig fetched from my crowded sty.
All dressed in white I'll walk behind   40
And bring the basket, myrtle - bound,

My head tied 'round with myrtle too -
So please your grace.

Let others play the gallant legionnaire.
Cut down, beneath the war god's smile,   45
The foremost foe, so each can tell
The deeds he did, a military man,
And as I drink, map out in wine
Campaigns upon a table cloth.
What is the madness then, I ask,   50
Provoking death, black death in war,
When, come what may, it threatens us
And comes, unseen, on silent feet?

There are no crops below, no grapes are grown;
But Cerberus, the insolent,   55
And the foul sailor of the Styx.
And there a bloodless crowd, with cheeks all torn
And hair that's blackened in the fire,
Wanders toward the shrouded lakes
That lie beyond our view.   60

He should sooner have our praise
Whom sluggish age takes captive in his hut,
Beside the children he has raised.
He gathers in the sheep himself,
His son the lambs; his wife prepares   65
Warm water when he's weary with his toil.
The life for me!
I hope my head will glow with white,
An aged man who tells his tales
Of days gone by. 'Til that time come,   70
I pray that Peace may grace our fields;
For it was Peace, yes, shining Peace
That first brought bulls beneath the yoke
To plough the land, and Peace that nourished vines
And stored the vintage. Jars a father sealed   75
Would run with wine for son.
In peace, the two-edged plough shines bright,

But in dark lofts the rust grows thick
Upon the sorry battle gear
Some leathery veteran hung away.   80

From picnic groves the tipsy farmer then
With wagon drives his wife and children home;
And then the wars of love grow hot. His wife
Laments torn hair, forced entry by her man,
And weeps for bruises on her tender cheeks;   85
While he who's won weeps too for the strength
Of hands gone mad, and wanton Love
Provides their brawl with fighting words,
While seated, stubborn spirit, in between.
He's stone, he's steel who strikes his own sweet girl.   90
He topples gods themselves out of the sky.
Enough to tear a scanty gown off limbs,
Enough to untie ribbons in her hair.
Enough to make her cry. The man whose rage
Can bring on tears in tender girls   95
Is four times blessed, but he whose hands are cruel
Should wield a spear, should wear a shield,
Stay far from love which is a gentle thing.

Come, Peace, Restorer, come to us,
An ear of corn held in your hand,   100
And let your shining bosom, Peace,
Teem with tumbling fruit.

Commentary

What is the nature of human aggressive impulses? What are their
origins and their effects, and how are we to respond to them? These are
the questions posed in this elegy. As we have seen, the poem begins
with a question about the most brutal form of human aggression, war.
How could any man have been cruel enough to initiate it? The poet
responds to this question with his first hypothesis about violence:
warfare is a perversion of man's natural instinct for self-preservation, his
response, specifically to the threat posed by wild animals. The
perversion of this instinct is then attributed to greed. It is the desire for

unnatural and superfluous wealth that was responsible for the use of deadly weapons against fellow human beings, and this use rendered man as wild as the beasts and as hard as the weapons he fashioned.

The lines that follow provide the reader with the poet's personal reaction to human aggression and war, a reaction with which we are already familiar. He longs for the simple rural life, free of ostentation and wealth and marked by ancient piety and ritual. This is, of course, the life that is fostered by peace, the opposite pole in the poet's antithetical paradigm of human existence, the pole which will become in this elegy a major motif and the precondition of the pastoral utopia which he once again visualizes. This pastoral life of peace is inscribed in the images which follow, all of them soft and sweet: flowers, fruits and honey, flocks of sheep and tender children, all of them in stark contrast with the images with which the poem opened.

In the central portion of the poem, the poet abandons his earlier modes of expression: exclamation, question, answer and prayer, and turns instead to vow. He promises to sacrifice to the Lares if they will protect him against the enemy. The vow completed, he then considers the two possible outcomes that the granting and the rejection of the vow by the Lares will bring about. He considers the outcomes of war first, beginning with an almost attractive vision of the aging veteran of the battlefield boasting over his wine of his youthful accomplishments. But the swaggering reminiscences of this elderly braggart soon give way to what the poet sees as the real outcome of war. The picture of the lone veteran is replaced by one of the poems most striking images in which the thousands killed in war are seen trooping through the underworld to their final resting places.

The poet then turns to the other pole to complete the contrast. The life of peace seems indeed all sweetness and light at first. First of all, that life is long and in it the throngs that stand beside one are not the dead but one's family. Like the warrior, the peacetime farmer also has his tales to tell, but his are tales of planting and herding, ploughing and making wine, the fostering rather than the destruction of life.

Then, quite suddenly, this idyllic vision of rural happiness is spoiled. The poet describes the behavior of a drunken farmer who is returning home from a rustic celebration. Under the influence of wine and with the assistance of Cupid or Love, he attacks his wife, tearing her hair, scratching her face and making her cry. The poet points out that such behavior is akin to that of the soldier, and so it appears that the roots of aggression are not, perhaps, as simply explained as he had suggested earlier in the elegy. Venus herself provokes her own kind of violence and her son provides the means for committing it. The roots of aggression do not lie in the perversion of our instinct for self-preservation alone; they spring, the poet suggests here from our sexual drives as well. Not surprisingly then, in the passage which describes the drunken farmer's love-making, the soft images of Peace become confused with brazen and flinty images of war.

The elegy concludes on a typically elegiac note of ambiguity. Even Peace can bring violence of a kind, if a man gives free rein to what is lowest in his nature. The poet is therefore obliged to end with both a command and yet another prayer, a command to men to control their base instincts in Love's service, and a prayer to Peace, calling upon her to come to him as a fostering and nurturing spirit of fruitfulness, untouched by violence bred of passion. Let Peace be mother and not seductress, and in that guise, make possible the dream world of the poet's imagination.

✦ ✦ ✦

2.1

Introduction

In this first elegy of his second book Tibullus speaks in three voices: as a farmer-priest conducting a religious ritual, as master of the feasting and revelry which follows it and as poet inspired by his godlike patron, Messalla and his exploits and achievements. The voices are not clearly distinguished and the reader must, therefore, be attentive to the transitions in the poem and to the fact that this blurring of role boundaries serves the further purpose of giving the entire poem an elevated religious and liturgical tone.

At the beginning of the elegy the poet's voice is heard as he addresses, perhaps at the head of a rustic chorus, the assembled local folk and their divinities. The community is celebrating the annual ritual purgation of the fields which was known as the *Ambaravalia,* and so, quite naturally, Ceres, the goddess of corn, and Bacchus, the god of fertility and of wine, are invited to the religious observance being conducted. The traditional instructions about behavior and dress are given to the participants, and then the poet describes the ceremony itself. We see the sacrificial animal approaching the altar and hear the prayers for healthy flocks and for a good harvest. Interestingly, the sacrifice of the animal itself is omitted and the poet passes on to the examination of the victim's entrails, which, he announces, promise the fulfillment of the people's prayers.

When the religious ceremony is finished, the poet assumes his second role, calling for the beginning of the feast and ordering both local Italian wine, Falernian, and wine imported from the Greek island of Chios. Then, as the drinking begins, he calls for a toast to his own absent patron, Messalla, who, as a member of the Arval Brotherhood, was probably conducting a similar ceremony in Rome on that very day. The toast to Messalla is a pivotal point in the elegy, for immediately after it, the poet begins to speak in the voice of a poet under Messalla's inspiration, reciting a hymn to civilization that touches upon its origins in the countryside as well as upon its advances and benefits. This poem-within-a-poem resonates with the poet's dual role as both farmer and bard, for it moves from the material benefits of civilization, food, tools and housing, to those that are spiritual and aesthetic, music and tragedy. In the case of tragedy, we are given a brief account of the origins of the genre in the *dithyramb* or hymn to Dionysus/Bacchus, an account which also alludes to the derivation of the word "tragedy" itself from, as many believe, the Greek word for goat, the animal awarded to the winner in early tragic competitions.

The last blessing of civilization mentioned by the poet is love. He moves gracefully to this theme, first describing boys and girls engaged in artistic pursuits such as the weaving of garlands and clothing. After introducing these youthful figures, he turns to Cupid and recalls that he too was born in the countryside. His first conquests, we are told, were in the fields among animals, but now, alas, he turns his bow against men and women as well. As an example of the results of this, the poet paints a vivid and moving scene in which a young girl gropes her way through a dark street at night on her way to visit her lover.

And the lovers' night becomes suddenly the night which frames the elegy. Time has passed in the text, and the bright sunlight which illuminated the early ceremony has disappeared with the coming of evening. Now the poet becomes master of the feast once again and addresses the throng of merrymakers. What he says is not, however, unrelated to the final amatory theme of the poem-within-a-poem, for he calls upon the folk to pray that the herds will multiply and flourish, and to pray as well for their own loves' fulfillment. Night, he warns as he closes, is coming and with it sleep and black dreams.

Translation

> Whoever is here today,
> Be reverent in your heart
> And gracious with your words.
> We're purifying fields and crops

The way our fathers did -   5
A rite that's generations old.

Lord Bacchus, come,
Horns hung with mellow grapes;
And Ceres, bind your brow with spikes of corn.
In holy light the earth should rest,   10
And rest the ploughman, heavy work
Put by and share hung high
Upon the wall. Untie the yokes,
For oxen too have earned the right
To stand, heads wreathed, before the brimming trough. 15
All things should be in service to the god.

So let no woman dare to place
A spinner's hand upon the wool;
And you on whom love lavished joy last night,
Stand far apart from altar's fire;   20
The chaste are the gods' delight. Come wearing white.
Draw water from our spring with hands unstained.

Now see, a lamb, the victim marked,
Goes to the glistening altar, crowds behind
All dressed in white, hair bound with olive leaves.   25
My fathers' gods, we cleanse the fields,
We cleanse the folk, and pray you drive
All evil from our walls,
Not let our crops deceive the scythe with weeds,
Not let the lamb, whose feet are slow,   30
Be frightened by the swifter wolves.
The well-fed farmer beams contented then
And trusts his fields, thick-grown and high,
Brings stouter logs to a glowing hearth.
The children of his slaves in swarms -   35
A sign the farm is flourishing -
With twigs play building houses at the fire.
The things I pray for will come true.
Look now, how fine the omens are,
How prophet entrails tell the gods are pleased.   40

Falernian for me,
Old vintage of the smoke-tinged grape.
Uncork the Chian and let our wine
Add savor to this special day.
Don't blush to drench your wits on holidays,   45
To strike a crooked course with feet that stray.
All now, cups high and say:
"Messalla's health," and let the toasts,
Each one by one, pronounce the name
Of him we miss, Messalla, famed   50
For triumphs won in Aquitania,
Messalla, victor, mighty boast
Of bearded ancestry as well.

Come now, be inspiration while this,
My song, gives thanks to country gods.   55
These fields and fields' divinities
I make my verse. Life learned from them
The way to drive its hunger off
With more than acorns from the oak;
And they were the first to teach   60
The art of joining beams, to roof
Our cottages with fresh cut thatch. It's said
They were the first to teach the bulls to serve,
To fix a wheel beneath a wagon's load.
Then scavenging for food gave way. Fruit-bearing trees   65
Were sown and fertile gardens drank
The water men brought near. Then golden grapes
Gave us the drink our feet did press,
And sober water mingled with the wine
That drives our cares away. Now country fields   70
Bear crops and every year,
Beneath the burning sunstar's heat,
The earth is shorn, spreads out its golden crest,
And light-winged bees in country fields
Bring pollen to their springtime hives   75
And work to fill sweet-honied combs.

Some farmer for the first time then

When he had had his fill of ploughing
Dawn to dusk, sang country songs,
And singing, kept a rhythmic beat.   80
He was the first, with supper done,
To pipe upon a brittling stalk and hymn
The gods whose images he'd decked with flowers.
A farmer, Bacchus, was the first,
His skill untried, to lead *your* dance and stain   85
His cheeks all red with cinnabar.
He was the man they gave the gift
Worth telling of; from teeming fold
They took it: he-goat, leader of the flock,
That made his meager holding grow.   90
In country fields a boy first wove
A crown of springtime flowers
And placed them on the ancient household gods.
In country fields the glistening sheep
Bear on their backs soft coats of wool: 95
A sign of work for girls
As yet in childhood's years.
That's where a woman's labor lies:
Her wool and distaff, spindle twisting threads
Beneath her thumb, for hours long   100
Minerva's devotee, singing
To the clatter of the loom,
As swinging brick-weights slap
Together while she weaves.

They say that Cupid's birth was in the fields,   105
Among the flocks; wild horses there;
And there his training with his novice bow.
But now - how skilled his hands have grown.
He hunts no cattle now as once before,
But takes delight in wounding girls   110
And humbling swaggering males.
He drains a young man's fortune now,
Commands old men, who'll sit and sit
Before a petulant sweetheart's door,
To speak all kinds of shameful rot.   115

And he's the guide when in the dark,
A girl, alone, comes out to meet her love
And like a thief hops over sleeping guards.
Tip-toed in fear she finds her way on foot
And gropes through pitch-black streets with
    outstretched hands.   120
Poor fools, whom Love drives hard, and happy he
On whom a peaceful Love breathes gently.

Hallowed Lord, come join our festal meal.
Put down your arrows, please, and hide
Your flaming torches far away.   125
Good people, sing the praise,
The praise of this, our famous god.
Pray to him for your flocks, aloud,
And each one softly for himself;
Or out loud too, for laughing crowds   130
Have raised a din. The buxom pipe
Echoes with a Phrygian tune;
So have your fun and take your sport.
Night yokes its horses now
And in a playful band flame-yellow stars   135
Now dance behind their mother's car.
Behind them come hushed sleep,
Curtained by its dusky wings,
And dreams, black dreams,
That move on stumbling feet.   140

Commentary

We have before us, as we have seen, a complex text in which the
voices of a farmer/priest, a master of the revels and a poet are cleverly
interwoven. It falls into three parts, each clearly recognizable by
syntactical markers. The lines in which the priest and master of the feast
appear are driven by exhortation, by the extensive use of subjunctive and
imperative verbs. In these sections the reader, who becomes a
surrogate for the peasant community, is drawn into the scene being
depicted by the commands and exhortations of the text. In the central
part of the text, the poem-within-a-poem, the narrative is carried largely
by indicative past-tense verbs, which serve to distance the reader from

its historical account of the evolution of civilization. This narrative portion of the text provides in this way a reflective and meditative core that operates upon the reader at some remove from the urgency suggested by the verbal insistence in the other sections. As we read the poet's account of the rise of civilization, we are made aware of the deeper significance of both the ritual and the revel in which we are exhorted to participate.

The elegy is, therefore, more than a mere depiction of a charming rural holiday and the events that marked it in the Roman world of the first century B.C. The poem is in fact a meditation upon the elemental and irrational forces that pervade human existence and upon human attempts to control or at least accommodate them. These attempts take the form, of course, of civilization, which is the subject of the poem-within-a-poem, and which is symbolized in the first part of the text by the religious ceremony being conducted, the purification of the fields and crops, and of the elemental powers which drive their cyclic renewal and fertility. The text does not, we should note at once, privilege civilization and ritual at the expense of the elemental and irrational. Both powers are given their due and left, at the elegy's conclusion in a delicate, perhaps even precarious balance.

In addition to the shift in voice and the use of the syntactic markers alluded to above, Tibullus depends heavily on both imagery and evolutionary history to structure his treatment of the confrontation between the elemental abyss and civilization. The imagistic media employed involve contrasts between light and darkness, between sounds, especially musical sounds, both implicit and explicit, and between kinds of movement. Let us explore these images and their use further.

As we have noted in the introduction above, this elegy begins in the realm of ritual and light. The ritual is itself a metaphor for civilization and it begins in the morning in bright sunlight which is specifically referred to as holy. The movement of this part of the text is the movement of a procession, slow, orderly and sedate. It is accompanied by the very choral hymn which the farmer/priest is leading, and from it are banished all elemental forces and the impurities which these produce. Participants in the ritual must be clothed in white and be free of the stains which both sexual activity and manual labor produce. Interestingly, even the ritual slaughter of the sacrificial victim is not explicitly described, but must be inferred by the reader from the reference to the animal innards which are read by the officiating priest.

Only conditionally do references to the elemental and irrational make an appearance in the earlier portion of the elegy. They appear, for example, in a negative context: in the prohibitions of weeds and wolves and of sexual passion. Significantly, Bacchus, the Roman counterpart of Dionysus, the god of passion and fertility, is invoked at once. He is invoked, however, as a god of sweetness and light, decked out with the fruits of his fertility, or perhaps better of his controlled and civilizing power. Indeed, the manner in which he is presented provides a key to understanding the poet's view of the relationship between elemental forces and civilizing ritual. The very essence of ritual is its ability to sanctify and purify cosmic forces which are at root irrational and terrifying.

A change in mood and perspective occurs with the completion of the ritual and the beginning of the revelry which follows it. Here, elemental and irrational forces are not only recognized but given admission to the festivities as well. Wine, Bacchus' gift, is called for, and the poet confesses that some degree of drunkenness is no disgrace on such a holiday. Indeed, the image which signifies this permission to tipple, reverses the orderly and sedate movement of the procession, and depicts the unsteady footsteps of a drunken reveler.

Sound imagery changes as well. First we hear the calling out of the toasts to Messalla over the cups of Falernian and Chian, far less sedate than the hymn that preceded them; and then we hear yet another kind of music, the poet's poem-within-a-poem, his hymn to the rise and evolution of civilization in the country. This extended poetic commentary on the events in which the reader is participating vicariously employs a largely historical frame, which traces the development of civilization from its early provision of material comforts like food and shelter, to the material and spiritual gift of wine and finally to the aesthetic boon of music, tragedy and the arts. In tracing the progress of civilization, the poet has brought us to that place where the elegy itself began, to the pure realm of liturgy and art, to the dithyrambic hymn to Dionysus, which echoes the hymn of the farmer priest which we have just heard.

Tibullus' poetic commentary does not close here however. In the final section of the poem-within-a-poem, Cupid, the offspring of Venus herself, is celebrated as yet another creature of the rustic countryside. He is seen at once as an irrational force that subjects men and women to the elemental power of passion. We see here that the commentary is taking the same course as the festival that is the subject of the elegiac text. The elemental, having been purified, has returned to claim its due, and the imagery of the text is altered to accommodate it. The final image of the poem-within-a-poem is that of a young girl, groping her way unsteadily through the darkness, driven by love to meet her illicit lover. The sexual drives which, the text emphasizes, humans share with the animal world, must be recognized; art and ritual can never entirely control the elemental.

As the internal poet's voice falls silent and we are returned to the revel itself, the same thematic movement occurs. Night is approaching and the proceedings are shrouded in darkness. The feast has become a raucous affair, filled with laughter and sensual Phrygian music. The master of the revel turns the thoughts of the revelers to procreation and fertility, first to the procreative activity of the animals, then to human passion and longing. The imagery continues to change. Light recedes to the stars whose movement is described as gay and wanton. Sleep, which will wrap the mind in darkness, approaches now, and with it the final metaphor for the irrational, black dreams. In short, Tibullus has, by the end of the elegy, brought us to the edge of the abyss, the very abyss with which the civilized ritual he depicted was designed to cope and coexist.

Many of Tibullus' favorite techniques inform this text: the manipulation of the poetic or lyrical voice and the use of both syntactic forms and imagery as structural markers. But something new has also appeared. Here, the reader is drawn into a poetic moment, the ritual and feast, a part of which is an internal commentary in the form of a hymn, whose referent is that moment itself. The event and the commentary on the event move along parallel axes and resonate with one another, and the reader, who responds vicariously to the exhortations of the priest and master of the revels, understands his responses in terms of the lesson given by the internal poet in the poem-within-a-poem.

✦   ✦   ✦

2.2

Introduction

The poet is attending the birthday celebration of his friend Cornutus. Although such a celebration had, for a Roman, greater religious significance than the modern birthday party, it did include the practice of making a wish for the future, and this feature of it is central to this elegy. As in the preceding poem, the poet himself assumes the role of officiating priest, exhorts the guests to assume a reverent attitude and calls upon the appropriate divinities or spirits. Two names are given to these, and indeed, it is difficult to know whether two separate spirits are being invoked or whether the names signify two aspects of the same supernatural presence. On the one hand, a single statue seems to represent them both; on the other, the poet clearly bids one to be present after already stating that the other is coming. The first spirit addressed is *Natalis*, the birth spirit, which presided over the birth of a child and which, quite naturally, was invited to return to the celebration of that birth each year. The *Genius*, also present at birth, was, on the other hand the individual's abiding spirit, a personification of his character and his protector throughout life. Whether these were seen as separate beings or two aspects of the same spirit, represented by a single image, is perhaps not an important issue. What is important, however, is that the two names signify different functions.

After calling for reverent silence, the poet presides over the religious formalities: the burning of incense, the adorning of the spirit's statue, the anointing of its temples with nard and finally the offering of ceremonial cakes and wine. This formal ritual then gives way to a lighter mood as we reach the moment at which Cornutus is called upon to make his wish.

Apparently he has difficulty making a suitable wish, and so the poet
himself gracefully and wittily comes to his rescue, suggesting first that
the statue has already nodded its assent to the prayer that is to be made
and then making the prayer himself on Cornutus' behalf. Cornutus, he
tells us, prays for the undying love of a faithful wife, something that he
would rather have than anything else in the world. The wish is granted,
the poet assures the others present and then, acting as prophet, he looks
ahead to the enduring love that lies in store for his friend and for its
long-term result: the reappearance of the Birth Spirit at the birth of
Cornutus' grandchildren.

How serious is this poem? How serious is the wish? Most of Tibullus'
critics agree that Cornutus must be seen as not yet married, for if a wife
were present, a prayer for her fidelity could easily suggest that the poet
entertained some doubts about her faithfulness. Was a fiancee present
perhaps? Might not the same inference be made about her? Is it
possible that Cornutus was in fact still sowing his wild oats and
somewhat reluctant to marry? In that case the poet might be speaking
in part in jest, in part, perhaps, on behalf of an anxious family concerned
about the production of offspring. We may not be able to answer this
question with certainty, but the poem's very ambiguity, which may be
intentional, deserves our consideration in the commentary which follows.

Translation

> Speak good thoughts only.
> The Birthday Spirit makes its way
> To our altar now.
> So everyone who's here, men, women, all,
> Be gracious with your tongues.   5
> Let holy incense burn upon our fire;
> Let burn perfumes
> That pampered Arabs send us
> From their wealthy land.
>
> And let his Genius come to see   10
> His honors, Genius on whose holy locks
> Soft garlands gracefully are hung.
> Now let his temples drip
> With undiluted scent and let him have

His fill of sacrificial cakes,   15
Washed down with pure unwatered wine.

Then let him grant, Cornutus,
Anything that you may ask.
Come now, why reticent?
The granting is already done. Just ask,   20
Or let me play the prophet now:
A wife's undying love is what you'll ask.
I'll bet the gods themselves know that.
You'd rather have her love
Than fields anywhere   25
That some brave farmer ploughs
Behind his sturdy ox.
You'd rather have it than the gems
That spring to life in fecund India,
Where waves upon the eastern sea   30
Are touched with red.

Your prayers have all been heard.
See how the god of love flies near
On wings that whir upon the wind
And bring you marriage chains of gold,   35
Chains meant to last forever - or
At least until old halting age
Brings wrinkles to your face
And streaks your hair with gray.
Then let the Birthday Spirit come again,   40
Provide grandparents with grandchildren then,
A sweet new whirl of children
To scamper at your feet.

Commentary

This brief elegy, which seems at first nothing more than an occasional piece, a birthday poem, what the Greeks called a *genethlakion,* the Romans a *carmen natale,* is perhaps more than that. Why should we suspect this? Why not simply accept the text as a piece of occasional verse written to oblige a friend, a witty greeting meant to serve much the same purpose as a birthday card? One should, of course, accept it as that, but there are, I would suggest, reasons for examining it more closely. First we should note that the elegy was not sent and forgotten. It was in fact included in the poet's collection of his works, most of which have greater significance than a mere birthday greeting. Second, we need to remember that as a poet, deeply influenced by the tradition of Hellenistic poetry, both Greek and Roman. Tibullus subscribed to the idea that even the seemingly insignificant events in life could be used to carry profound meaning. Finally, the text itself poses a number of puzzles that suggest that more may be going on in it than its surface displays to the inattentive reader.

Three things deserve our special attention. First, we should ask why Tibullus chose to introduce not a single or simple divinity or spirit, but, as we have seen, either two such figures or at least a figure that has two faces, both that of the Birthday Spirit and that of the Genius. Next we must surely confront the somewhat peculiar behavior of Cornutus himself, who is reluctant to make his own birthday wish, and who thereby forces the poet to make a wish for him, a wish about marriage, which is, in fact, a rather strange subject for elegiac verse. Finally we should remark upon the pervasiveness of imagery dealing with the opulent and exotic, which furnishes a kind of bass accompaniment to the treble of the ecphrastic treatment of the ceremony being conducted.

The distinction between *Natalis* and *Genius* is, I think, important. The Birthday Spirit is a personification of a universal power which participates and drives procreation. It returns again and again, in generation after generation, as the elegy itself notes. One's own Birthday Spirit is, in this sense, larger than one's self; it is part of the life spirit of the race and the community themselves. If it speaks to the individual, it delivers an imperative: the command to participate with it in the preservation of the human race and of the members of an individual family or society. The Genius, on the other hand, is unique to the individual, personifying, as it does, his or her character and the acts and accomplishments that character has produced. The imperatives of the Genius and the Birthday Spirit may therefore differ, for one is universal, the other particular.

This elegy opens and closes with the Birthday Spirit and appropriately so, for the Birthday Spirit returns again and again both to the celebrant and to his descendants. The center of the elegy is occupied, however, by the Genius, who comes specifically to behold the deeds and honors of the celebrant, Cornutus, to see, in short, what his character has produced and is producing. What the Genius sees is in fact a young man somewhat irresolute, not yet determined perhaps to make life's crucial choices and to undertake what for a Roman was his central obligation: to assure that the family survives by marrying and producing offspring, the natural results of an enduring marriage. The poet's bantering exchange with Cornutus can be taken as good fun, but it is also perhaps admonitory. It may in fact be saying that Cornutus' Genius is in someway a disappointment to his friends and family. Is there not perhaps something in Cornutus' life that is getting in the way of his shouldering his procreative responsibilities, and, if so, what is it?

It has not been noted, I think, that the statue which represents the Genius enjoys extravagant honors. Not just any incense is burned, but incense that carries the perfumes of Arabia. This is a strong initial image and it is reinforced by subsequent images of opulent extravagance: the dripping temples, the rich meal of cakes and the deep draughts of unwatered wine. It is, in fact, the personification of Cornutus, his character that is treated this way in the text; and then, when the poet himself makes Cornutus' wish, he takes pains to point out that Cornutus would want a faithful wife even more than acres of land and the gems that lie in exotic India. What the imagery is telling us, it seems to me, is that the Genius of Cornutus has been seduced by the opulent and exotic, and that on the celebration of his birth, he must be reminded that the Birthday Spirit, is calling him to a higher obligation and work. In short, *Natalis* and *Genius* must become once again a single power. The nodding of the statue signifies its own desire for this reintegration through Cornutus' mature acceptance of his responsibilities.

The significance, then, of this seemingly slight piece of verse goes beyond the occasion which it records and celebrates. Its elegiac world draws the reader's attention to a fundamental contradiction in human affairs: that the drive to procreate and the individual *persona* are often at odds, that concern for self and a delight in luxury impede familial and communal obligation. And it is precisely the birthday, at which the *Natalis* appears again and again, that brings the age, wisdom and maturity that resolves that contradiction.

✦ ✦ ✦

2.3

Introduction

This elegy, like the one which precedes it, is addressed to Cornutus, and since there is no reason to doubt that the two addressees are in fact the same individual, we will need to consider why Tibullus chose to address this poem to someone who, on the surface at least, has little or nothing to do with its contents.

A second question of identity also needs to be considered in discussing this poem, which is not an occasional piece, but yet another lover's lament, directed this time at a woman who is identified late in the text as Nemesis. *Nemesis* is a Greek term which can be translated as righteous indignation, the cause of indignation or the vengeance which follows indignation. In Greek mythology, Nemesis is a goddess who avenges by bringing punishment to those who have acted outrageously. Given the derivation of the name and the late appearance of it in this, the first elegy in which it appears, we ought also to consider whether the woman referred to in the second book of elegies is someone other than the Delia of the first book or whether she is simply a later version of Delia who has been given a new and significantly bitter nick-name. Students of Tibullus have traditionally taken Nemesis to be a second, later love of the poet, but there is no conclusive evidence that this is the case. It is true that the characterization of Nemesis is considerably more negative, but this may simply indicate that the poet has grown more disillusioned and angry. There are, in fact, several reasons for assuming that the two figures are one and the same woman: both have sophisticated and expensive taste, both are involved with a rich rival and both employ the services of a suspicious bawd to arrange their love affairs. We should not, therefore, leap to a conclusion about the woman's identity as we approach the text, but, as with the presence of Cornutus, reserve judgement and return to the question in the commentary that follows.

Whoever Nemesis may be, we find at the beginning of the elegy that she has left Rome to visit the vast estate of a wealthy lover, where she is now being kept, perhaps, although this is not certain, not entirely willingly. In a state of depression and despair, the poet turns to his friend Cornutus and makes his lament, which contains a series of emotional outbursts and extravagant solutions to his problem. First, noting that Venus and her son Amor or Cupid have themselves moved to the country, the poet suggests that he too will follow not, as in earlier poems, to play the role of wealthy gentleman farmer, but to work as a lowly ploughboy, toiling for his hated rival - all this simply to be able to see his love. Is such a strategy even to be contemplated? Yes, the poet insists, for even the sun god Apollo, referred to here as Phoebus as well, served in such a capacity on the farm of Admetus whom he loved. To emphasize this point, the poet gives us a vivid tableau in which he depicts the toil and suffering of the god and the unhappy consequences of his servitude. He dwells upon Apollo's unkempt appearance, the failure of his arts, the indignities he was forced to endure, the grief of his sister Diana, who was born together with him on the island of Delos, and of their mother Leto, and finally the neglect of his famous shrine at Delphi where his priestess Pytho proves unable in his absence to pronounce the oracles which pilgrims to the shrine expect to receive.

His anger once again gets the better of him, however, and in a passage from which unfortunately some lines are missing, he appears to lash out once again at his wealthy rival. The man's extravagance provokes him further and he takes up once again what is by now a familiar theme: his age's inordinate greed and the lengths to which men will go to accumulate vast wealth, only to squander it on land and houses, fish ponds and expensive tableware. Then, all at once, he's brought up short again. He reminds himself that even Venus, Goddess of Love, longs for wealth. Very well, then, he concludes, he will bring his Nemesis back to the city and surround her with luxury himself, provide her with silks from the island of Cos, with slaves from India and purple garments from Africa and Tyre. Will this in fact work? No, he admits, his rival, that former slave, who once had to mount the block and, to demonstrate his fitness to prospective masters, lift his chalked feet in a trot, is now as wealthy as a king and beyond competition. What can the poet do but curse him and his land, praying to Bacchus to destroy his vintage?

Now, in a reversal of his frequent praise of civilization and agriculture, the poet continues his tirade by renouncing his own civilized age. For a brief interlude he pictures himself beside his Nemesis in a primitive Edenic world, enjoying the free food the trees spontaneously provide and the free love that no locks and guards prohibit. Rather this rough uncivilized life, he exclaims, than being without his love. Even this, however, is an illusion, an unrealizable fantasy, and so, as the elegy draws to a close, he returns to the strategy with which it opened. He will return to the country and toil as a slave, so long as he can be near his love. With a vision of this grim prospect, the poet brings his harangue to a close.

Translation

> Some country house has got my girl,
> Cornutus, yes, some big estate,
> And, oh, that man's an iron man
> Who still lives in the town,
> When even Venus has just moved away   5
> And lives in open fields;
> And Love, a rustic, learns to speak
> The words the ploughboys use. *→ to be a ploughboy*
>
> But oh, if I could gaze upon my love,
> How bravely there I'd turn black soil   10
> And man the sturdy two-tined hoe,
> A farmer, walk behind a bent-grip plough,
> As oxen furrowed seed land there.
> And no complaint from me,
> If sun should burn my slender limbs,   15
> Or broken blisters mar my hand's soft skin.
> One time, Apollo, handsome god,
> Fed Lord Admetus' bulls.
> His lute gave no divine advantage then,
> No help his hair in curls.   20
> Nor could he heal his woe
> With balm from herbs, for love

Had conquered all the medicine he knew.
So god himself grew used to driving cows
From stalls ***** and learned to mix   25
The rennet with fresh pails of milk,
Until, in mixing, milk grew hard.
Then he wove a basket
With tender shoots of rush, with holes
Within the weave to let the whey run through.   30
How often, so the story goes,
His sister blushed to meet him in the fields,
A calf around his neck. How often too,
As he sat singing deep within some dale,
Did cattle, mooing, interrupt   35
His graceful, mind-full, tune. Great captains came
That year, with fortunes tottering,
For oracles they came and left his shrine,
A mob unblessed by his reply.
And often mother Leto stared   40
In horror and in grief for holy locks
That step-dame Juno once admired.
Whoever saw his unwreathed head,
His curls unset, did wonder then
What had become of Phoebus' hair.   45
Where, Phoebus, is your Delos now?
Where Delphi, Pytho too? It seems that love
Commands a smaller dwelling now.
Yes, happy once, undying gods,
They say, served Venus openly   50
And felt no shame, while now
Of Phoebus' plight how others talk!
Still anyone who's smitten by a girl
Prefers the talk to being god
Without his love.   55

And you, no matter who you are,
Whom Cupid bids with scowling looks
To stage invasions of our house...
                    *****
This iron age holds out no praise

For love. It's profit that they praise,   60
Though profit works a multitude of ills.
It's profit girds a savage line
Of infantry with grating swords,
And then comes gore and then comes blood
And death becomes an instant thing.   65
It's profit makes a man take twice
The risk upon the vagrant sea
When battle prows are fitted
To his flimsy ships. The profiteer
Is hot to annex boundless land,   70
To pasture many acres
With his countless sheep. His mind is full
Of foreign stone: through city's din he moves
His columns with a thousand sturdy teams.
He closes in the untamed sea   75
With heaps of stones, so fish, meandering slow,
Can swim inside and pay no heed
To winter storms. But as for me,
Let jars of Samnian ware prolong
My happy feast, along with pliant clay   80
Some wheel at Cumae's shaped into a cup

And yet, I see girls love a millionaire.
Well then, come profit now,
If Venus really longs for opulence.
Let Nemesis, my Nemesis   85
Glide by in luxury,
Parade the town, a sight to see
In gowns she got from me. Sheer silks
She'll wear some woman wove on Cos,
In patterns with sewn avenues of gold;   90
And hers two dusky slaves
Whom India has scorched and stained -
So close the sun is driven
By his horses there. Let lands contend
To make a gift of choicest hues: 95
Vermillion sent from Africa
And purple sent from Tyre.

Pipe dreams, these things I say.
The man who had to jog the block
With slave's chalked feet - and not just once -   100
That man now has a kingdom of his own.
But as for you who lured my Nemesis
From town, you, stone-hearted Ceres,
May earth that's faithless pay
You back with seeds turned stone.   105
And you, o Bacchus, gentle Lord,
Who sows the merry grape, forsake
As well the vats that we have cursed,
For surely hiding pretty girls
In those depressing fields deserves   110
A punishment. No vintage, Father Bacchus,
Commands a price so high.

I want no part of farming, no-
Not as long as girls still grace the fields.
We'll dine on nuts for nourishment   115
And water will provide our drink
As in years past, for ancient men
Ate only nuts, and they made love
At any time, in any place.
What harm in having unsown fields?   120
A gentle Venus in those days
Gave joy to men, who felt love breathe
In shaded valleys, unconcealed.
There were no guards, no doors to keep
Sad lovers out. I pray, if pray I may,   125
The custom might return again.
                        *****
They might as well clothe shivering bodies
With a cloak that's rough. For if my love
Is cloistered now and seldom to be seen,
What pleasures lie for this poor man   130
In a toga's casual chic?
No, lead me out; I'll plough those fields
Beneath my mistress' tyranny,
And as her slave, refuse no whips,
Refuse no chains that love applies.   135

Commentary

This elegy treats unexpected and absurd reversals in human fortunes and sensibilities. Its voice is the voice of the desperate and distracted poet, who finds himself once again without his love, and it is addressed, to his friend Cornutus, who appeared in the preceding elegy and who, since he is named only once at the beginning of the poem, must be intended as a means of positioning the reader as he listens to the voice of the poet. As in earlier elegies the disordered mentality of the lovesick poet lends verisimilitude to the apparently disordered train of thought and to the seemingly abrupt transitions in the text. This disjointedness is, however, superficial only, for the elegy is in fact carefully constructed and its annular construction is clearly marked by linguistic and thematic anaphors. In the outermost rings of the poem the poet pictures himself as working as a farm laborer in order to catch glimpses of his beloved. Just inside these rings lie two rings which treat mythic antiquity, one a depiction of Apollo's servitude, the other a fantasy about retreating to a mythic golden age. At the center of the elegy lies the poet's reaction to his rival and all that he stands for: grasping greed and the manipulation of love through wealth. This section itself falls into three parts: a lament for this unnatural materialism in the rival and in others, a momentary resolve by the poet to mimic such behavior himself and thus to lure his love back to the city, and, when that strategy is seen to be hopeless, a prayer to the gods of agriculture to bring blight to the rival's fields and vines, itself a bold reversal of the poet's normal attitude to these divinities.

What we are presented with, then, is a world in which everything and everyone has been turned up-side-down. The beloved, who characteristically has been in the city while the poet is on his farm, is now on a farm while he remains in the city. The poet, a Roman citizen of means, contemplates working as a farmhand on the vast estate of a man who was once a slave. Apollo, a god, is recalled as having demeaned himself by slaving on the farm of his beloved, a motif which is developed in a long and comic passage about the effects of this metamorphosis: the mooing of cows while he sings, the shock and dismay of his relatives at his unkempt appearance and the shutting down of the oracle shop at Delphi. Even the poet's sensibilities are turned up-side-down, for at one point he contemplates using wealth himself to lure his love back to the city, and at another point he calls upon the gods to wither the crops of his rival, the very opposite of his customary prayers.

The world presented here is indeed a mad world seen through the surrealist lens of the desperate poet. To what end, we need to ask, is such a vision employed? I would suggest that we are once again dealing with Tibullus' enduring fascination with instability in human affairs and especially in human affairs of the heart. I would further suggest that this concern with instability also suggests the answer to the question raised above about the identity of Nemesis. Is Nemesis simply a new nickname for Delia or are we dealing with a second new love? The evidence is not conclusive, and, as we noted above, arguments can be advanced for either possibility. If, however, we locate the thematic center of this poem and of several which follow in the poet's concern for change and reversal, which reply to this question makes more sense? Surely the reversal is far more striking if the woman involved is the same woman, who because of changes in her own attitudes and behavior now bears a new and significant name. Perhaps, in the end, the question of identity need not be pushed too hard. Delia and Nemesis are after all textual figures, characters in Tibullus' elegiac world. As such, their primary identity must lie in the fact that they are the mistress or mistresses of the poet. In short, in terms of the thematic texture of the poems, the two women have the same poetic valence and are, therefore virtually interchangeable.

If then Tibullus is once again focusing on instability and change, why did he choose to address Cornutus here and how does this choice act to position his reader? We need to remember that the reader has just met Cornutus in the preceding elegy. He saw him as a young and immature young man for whom the poet had to suggest important decisions about life, decisions, in fact, which involved the young man's love life. In the public and religious setting in which the birthday elegy takes place, the poet chose to argue for a life of sexual steadfastness and fidelity, for a world in which human passion is unchanging. In the present elegy, the poet addresses Cornutus privately about his own very private concerns. He is not now bound by the proprieties the birthday party demanded be observed. He can, in fact, speak what he believes is so, not what ought to be so. The poem is, therefore, a kind of retraction or at least correction. In standing in the place of Cornutus, the reader allows himself to be further instructed. He hears the poet, once again in the role of *praeceptor amoris* or teacher of love, adding a chilling footnote to the discourse of the preceding poem.

We are here at the very center of Tibullus' elegiac world, a world which can be seen from many different perspectives and through many different lenses. It is a world, as we noted in the preface, that is bittersweet. What seems at once moment sweet, may in another seem bitter; what seems bitter in one place, may seem sweet in another. This is Tibullus' poetic vision, the basis of his elegiac lament. It is a vision very much in the tradition of the earlier Hellenistic poets of Greece, who are often his models and whose techniques he often uses. The world may be viewed in many ways: what seems heroic or divine may also be seen as human and even comic. Hence the importance and length of the treatment of Apollo in this elegy. The upside-down portrait of the handsome and sophisticated god as an unkempt and sweaty farmhand is emblematic of the elegists' sensibility and message. There is no stability in human life or knowledge of life; bitter becomes sweet, sweet becomes bitter; and this we should lament in Tibullus' bittersweet and ironic fashion.

✦   ✦   ✦

2.4

Introduction

In this elegy the poet's situation seems to have changed again. He is not, as in the preceding poem, completely separated from his love, who is, incidentally, identified as Nemesis only in the penultimate line of this poem; rather, he is able to see her from time to time. These approaches to her are, however, difficult, and the poet's state is now described as outright slavery. He imagines himself in chains, tormented by a mistress who applies torches to his suffering body, and his agony is so terrible that he longs to be changed into a rocky promontory that is worn down by the waves.

It is clear, however, that he is still excluded, this because Nemesis demands costly gifts as the price of admitting him. Nor is his poetry helpful. Although he writes only to win his love, eschewing both heroic and philosophical poetry, his elegies achieve nothing, and so, in frustration, he bids farewell to both Apollo, the god of poetry, and to the Muses, his source of inspiration. Better, he decides, to acquire the riches Nemesis demands through theft, and what more fitting theft than the pillaging of the temples of Venus, goddess of love, who is the cause of his distress?

Next, the frustrated poet shifts his attention from Venus, his divine scapegoat, to those who provide the extravagant objects that make girls greedy, whose enterprises produce the silk gowns from the island of Cos and the pearls from the Red Sea that women demand as the price of their favors. This is what turns love into a commercial transaction and what excludes lovers whose slender resources keep them from achieving the consummation of their desire. Indeed this transformation, he adds,

has even tarnished the reputation of Amor, the god of Love himself. At
this point the poet's attention returns to his own beloved. Still bitter, he
now curses her, praying that no one will come to save her burning house
and that no one will be present to weep at her grave. To Nemesis, a
paragon of greed, he then opposes the model wife who is free of avarice
and whose husband both weeps at her grave and returns each year to
offer flowers and prayers.

   As the elegy draws to a close, the poet acknowledges that his
moralizing is in vain. He must play at love by love's and his mistress'
rules, and so he decides that he will sell everything he has, risk
bankruptcy itself, auctioning off the very Lares, the gods of his house,
to provide Nemesis with the gifts she demands. And more than that, he
will accept her tyranny and gladly drink the poisons Medea and Circe,
mythology's legendary witches, brew, all the poisons produced in the
enchanted land of Thessaly in the north of Greece, even the aphrodisiac
secretions of mares in heat, if only Nemesis will gaze on him, her eyes
no longer on fire.

Translation

And so I see it's slavery for me;
A mistress has been trained in tyranny -
For me. And now good-bye
To the freedom that was mine from birth,
Dark prison-house of slavery mine,   5
Held fast by chains, those bonds
That Love will never loose
From these, my suffering limbs.
For me, deserving or untouched by sin,
Love fans his flames and I am - oh -   10
On fire. Cruel woman, take away
Those torches. Oh... if only I could
Numb myself to pains like these.
I'd rather be a stone
Upon some frigid peak, some crag   15
That stands exposed to raging winds,
Worn down by pounding ship-wreck waves
Beside the endless sea. Now day is bitter,
More bitter still the dark of night,

And every season drips with sickening gall.   20

My elegies afford no help,
No help Apollo, author of my song,
For still she comes, hands cupped, to ask her price.
Go, Muses, get away from me,
Unable as you are to help   25
A man in love. No worship that you have
From me has poems of war in view.
I sing no journeys of the sun,
Or how the moon, her orb now full, wheels round
Her horses and then hastens to return.   30
An easy way to reach my love -
That's what my songs are looking for.
So, Muses, go; get far away,
If singing has no power.

I'll have to find her gifts with daggers drawn,   35
Commit some crime to end this wallowing
In tears before her bolted house,
Steal votive tablets hanging in the shrines.
Let Venus then endure my rape
Before the other gods; it's she   40
Who sets me on to crime so foul.
It's she who consecrates a mistress
Who devours all I own, and so it's she
Deserves to feel my sacrilegious hands.

But death to him who gathers emeralds,   45
Colors pure white wool with Tyre's purple dye.
Here's the cause of greed in girls,
These gowns from Cos, the Red Sea pearls.
They turned them bad; *they* are the reason why
Our doors felt keys, why watch dogs took   50
Their posts before our gates.
But if the price is right, the guard gives way,
No locks obstruct your path.
The dogs themselves lie silent at your feet.
Whatever god gave beauty to a greedy girl,   55

Oh what a boon he brought,
On top of what a world of ill!
Then sobs rang out and lovers' quarrels,
And Love's become, because of this,
A god of doubtful sanctity.   60

But you who lock a lover out
For lack of gold, may wind and fire
Steal all the wealth that you've acquired.
I hope the local boys gaze gratified
Upon your house on fire and no one make   65
A move to douse the flames.
Your death will come, alas,
And no one there to weep or bring
The offerings to grace your gloomy rites.
But for the woman who is good   70
And free of greed, although she live
A hundred years, tears will be shed
Before the embers of her pyre.
And some old man, in honor
Of a lasting love, will bring fresh flowers   75
Year in, year out and place them on her tomb,
Then, parting say, "Rest well, in peace,
And may the earth sit light upon your bones
In death's untroubled sleep,"

My warning tells what's true,   80
But what have I to gain in truth?
We have to worship Love by rules
That she's made up and if she orders us
To sell our family home, then Lares,
Under orders off to sale you go.   85
Whatever poisons Circe has,
Medea too; whatever herbs
The land of Thessaly provides,
Whatever aphrodisiac
Drips down from mares in heat,   90
When Venus sends the wind of passion
Through the wild unmated herds,

A thousand brews she may concoct
From other herbs, and I will drink them all,
If only Nemesis, my Nemesis   95
Will look on me with eyes whose fire is stilled.

Commentary

Consider three questions about this elegy. First, why at the very beginning of the poem does the poet ask his mistress to take away the flames of her passion and why does he pray to be made as insensitive to passion as a rock beaten by the sea? Does this not seem to contradict the remainder of his lament, which rebukes Nemesis precisely for withholding her love because of the inadequacy of the poet's gifts? Second, why does the poet single out Venus, the goddess of love itself, as the object of his sacrilegious violation? Should he not here be asking her favor instead? Finally, why, at the conclusion of the poem, does the poet agree to drink poison, highlighting with what is arguably the most powerful image of the elegy, a concoction that is obviously an aphrodisiac? Is he suicidal? Does he want to be driven utterly mad with passion? Is he perhaps so deranged that he no longer knows what he wants? We have found, after all, that Tibullus often employs a poetic voice which implies an altered psychic state.

Explanations of the message encoded in this elegy's text usually begin, correctly I believe, with the recognition that the poem carries forward the themes of reversal and retribution that have been prominent in the second book of the collection. The situation of the poet and the images used to convey that situation all suggest reversal and contrast. The freeborn poet is now a slave. The flames of passion are so painful that he wishes to become a rock. Both his poetry and his role as teacher of the mysteries of love are now disparaged and foresworn, and he decides in fact to violate Venus herself. His world is a world upside-down in which women are no longer wept for at the grave, in which indeed no man who has experienced their avarice will even bring water to douse the flames of their burning houses. In short, the poet has reached the very nadir of love gone wrong, of passion disappointed and driven to despair. The mistress, whoever she is, has quite literally become his nemesis. The reversal of his situation represents the retribution which his mad love has earned.

The central portion of the text is perfectly clear about the ground of this reversal. The poet is unable to find fulfillment because of the avarice of his mistress. She comes to him with hands cupped, asking her price, and presumably, when he cannot pay it, she turns to the other lovers her procuress provides. This theme is carefully elaborated. The poet contemplates theft as a solution. He curses those who provide the rich gifts his mistress demands. He curses all greedy women everywhere, contrasting them with upright and faithful wives, and finally he agrees to accept any fate, poverty, even death perhaps, if only his Nemesis will look upon him with a peaceful gaze.

How much of this is new? The theme of material greed is certainly not. It appeared much earlier in the first book of elegies. Even there Delia was won away by the gifts of a wealthy rival. What accounts then for the poet's increasingly desperate state of mind? Why is he now *in extremis*? I would suggest that the answer to this question lies in the answer to the questions posed above. Although the center of the poem focuses upon a reversal brought about by material greed, the beginning and end of the poem suggest a more fundamental reversal, one based on sexual greed and uncontrolled passion. The flames which the poet prays to have removed as the elegy opens are in fact the flames of his mistress' own desire, which now outstrips even his own. In the light of this dramatic reversal, the guilt of Venus in the poet's eyes is quite understandable. He is now dealing with a woman whose passion he himself cannot quench, and who therefore turns to other lovers who are able to provide both material *and* sexual satisfaction. The aphrodisiac image at the poem's conclusion no longer seems as strange as it did when we first met it. The poet is in fact in need of an aphrodisiac. In this context, the references to the witches, Circe and Medea, also take on new meaning, for while one used her magic to assist in the theft of the golden fleece, the other used her poisons to turn men into swine. Finally, the last lines of the elegy take on a new significance. The peaceful gaze for which he longs is the gaze of woman whose passion has been satisfied and who will, therefore, remain faithful. The flames of that passion will now be withdrawn, as the poet asked earlier in his lament, and Venus and Love will once again be reputable gods.

As we have frequently found, the ironies in Tibullus' elegiac world run deeper than we imagine at first. The elegiac voice, although it dwells at length on the almost hackneyed theme of material greed, gives away the poet's deeper frustration at the elegy's beginning and end. The lover's passion, which seemed earlier in the collection a force scarcely able to be matched even by a rival, is, it seems, surpassed by the passion of his mistress herself, who must seek gratification in the arms of other lovers who bring her riches as well. Surely this is the most poetically just revenge. The retribution of Nemesis, whoever she may be, is both exquisite and ironic, for it turns love and desire themselves on their heads.

◆◆◆

2.5

Introduction

The poet is attending a ceremony at which his patron's son is being inducted into the priesthood of the *quindecimviri sacris faciundis*. This group of fifteen priests was one of the four major priesthoods in Rome and had the responsibility for keeping and consulting the books of Sibylline prophecies. It was open to the sons of prominent Roman families and, unlike the priesthood today, induction into it did not prevent its members from participating in other careers and activities, military, political, social and economic.

Messalla's son, Messallinus, was probably a relatively young man at the time of his induction. As the poem begins, we are meant to see him in the temple of Phoebus Apollo on the Palatine Hill. His family is gathered around him: his father, the great Valerius Messalla Corvinus, prominent among them and surrounded by his political friends and literary acquaintances. It is possible that the Emperor Augustus himself is present, although there is no evidence of this in the poem itself; and we need to remember that Messalla, although he fought for Augustus, was a man of strong republican sentiments.

The poet is also present. He is no doubt happy for his patron and proud of his patron's son, but, even as he prays, his mind wanders somewhat, as we shall see. He begins, of course, by praying to Apollo, in whose temple he finds himself, beseeching the god to be present and to look with favor upon his new priest. In making this prayer, the poet also evokes the image of Apollo which stood in the temple, Skopas' statue of the god playing the lyre, his long hair carefully arranged, his brow bound with laurel, his body draped in a flowing ceremonial gown.

As the celebrants pile their sacrifices on the altar, the poet praises the god's ability to reveal the future and recalls how he grants this power to others: to the augur who interprets the flights and songs of birds, to the haruspex who reads the entrails of sacrificial victims and, of course, to the Sibyl herself, whose prophecies the young Messallinus will care for as priest.

Who was the Sibyl? In the earliest references to her she appears, now in one place, now in another, as a single prophetess, who in a state of ecstasy utters prophecies to her priests, who then write them down in verse. Later, as many as ten or twelve different Sibyls are mentioned by ancient authors. One of them, Amalthea, dwelled at Cumae in Italy, and it is she, in the *Aeneid* of Vergil, who grants Aeneas permission to visit the underworld, she whose prophecies were in time acquired by the Romans and kept by the *quindecimviri*. These ancient books were, however, destroyed by fire in 83 B.C., and the Romans were forced to reassemble the collection from other prophetic texts. This may in fact explain the reference later in the elegy to other famous Sibyls: to Herophile of Marpesa, to Poeto of Samos and to the Sibyl of Tibur who, legend had it, swam across the river Anio east of Rome with the leaves of her prophecy concealed in her bosom, which was kept miraculously dry.

The poet closes his prayer to Apollo by asking that Messallinus be permitted, as a new priest, to approach and learn the Sibylline books. As the ceremony moves forward, however, his mind dwells not simply on the new priest but upon the Sibyl's revelations to the Romans and especially upon those given to Aeneas, the hero of the *Aeneid*, who fled from Troy with his father and their household gods and journeyed to Italy where he established the royal line that would in time found Rome. The poet meditates upon these events and upon the ancient site of Rome, which was, before the founding of the city, little more than rustic farmland. Delighted by this rural prospect, he pictures two of Rome's hills, the Palatine and the Capitoline, upon which the great temple of Jupiter would be built. He celebrates the rustic divinities, Pan and Pales and concludes his reverie with a charming vision of young people: a piping shepherd and a young girl who sails across the Velabrum, a marshy backwater of the Tiber, to visit her love.

His vision is, however, cut short, by the words once spoken by the Sibyl to Aeneas, words which were, in all likelihood, read aloud as part of the ceremony of induction that is taking place. In this utterance, the priestess reveals to the uncomprehending Aeneas what is in store for him and for his descendants: the Laurentian land in Italy on which he will build his first city, his own victory and deification at the river Numicius, the defeat of the indigenous Italians and their leader Turnus, his marriage to the local princess, Lavinia, and his son's founding of the city of Alba Longa, the forerunner of Rome. Finally the Sibyl predicts the seduction of the Vestal Virgin Ilia by Mars, the birth of her sons, Romulus and Remus, the founding of Rome itself and the growth of its empire. Then, swearing to the truth of her prophecy by her virginity, she falls silent.

The poet's mind continues to wander. He now considers the prophecy of other Sibyls, who predicted, he recalls, darker and more recent events, revealing all of the baleful omens which accompanied the civil wars of his own century and the assassination of Julius Caesar. What made him think of omens? He is watching the fire on the altar, of course, watching to see in its flames what omens Apollo will send now. And so, he drifts back to a private prayer, asking Apollo for omens of peace and abundance. This prayer leads him once again to envision one of his favorite poetic tableaux: common country folk enjoying the activities which peace brings, harvesting and celebrating the rural festivals dedicated to Bacchus and to Pales, gods of wine and herds, as they feast and play with their children. He dwells especially upon images of young people picnicking upon the grass, and this in turn leads him to another favorite theme, a squabble between a tipsy youth and his love. This vignette provokes yet another prayer to Apollo, a prayer beseeching the god to curb the activity of Cupid and especially to protect the poet himself in his sad love affair with his Nemesis.

Why should the god spare the poet? So that he can celebrate the great deeds of the new priest Messallinus. The poet even now imagines the young man's future triumphs and his father's pride in them. Will the god grant these prayers? The poet looks up at the statue, the very image with which the poem began, and asks it to nod in assent, promising as he does so to pray for the god's lovely hair and for the perpetual chastity of his sister divinity Diana.

Translation

> Phoebus, be kind.
> A new priest makes his way into your shrine.

Come now with lute, with songs come now,
And now, I beg, pluck strings that sing
And bend the words to fit the song   5
Of tribute I compose.
And with your temples bound
By laurel, triumph's flower, come,
Receive your holy rites,
As mortals pile your altars high.   10
Yes, come all bright and beautiful.
Today, put on the gown laid carefully aside.
Comb well today your long and flowing hair -
The way you looked - so men recall -
When Saturn fell, who was your king;   15
And you sang songs to Jupiter,
Victorious.
Far off, you see the things to come.
The augur, holy slave to you,
Knows well what fates the prophet birds do sing,   20
And lots which men consult obey your power.
The haruspex, through you, will feel
Foreboding, when the god has marked
The slippery bowels with signs.
The Sibyl, when inspired by you,   25
Has never worked deception
On the Romans, as she chanted
The hidden fates in six-beat verse.
Let Messallinus, Phoebus, touch
Your priestess' holy books.   30
I beg you, be his teacher then
Of what she prophesies.

She gave Aeneas signs of prophecy,
When, as the story goes, he'd borne
His father on his back, with the household gods   35
He'd snatched away. He had no faith
In a Rome to come, when in his grief he gazed
Across the sea to Troy, her gods in flames.
For Romulus had not yet shaped
The walls of this eternal town,   40

Walls never meant to house
Co-regent Remus in their round. Then cows
Did graze upon the grassy Palatine,
And on the Hill of Jove low huts did lie,
And Pan, still wet with votive milk,   45
Would linger there beneath a shady oak,
With Pales, whom some farmer's hook had shaped
In wood. And in a tree a gift hung high,
A wandering shepherd's querulous pipe,
All hallowed to the forest god,   50
A pipe whose reeds descend
In order, smaller, smaller still,
The shorter bound to longer stalks
With waxen bond. And where Velabrum lies
A little boat once made its way   55
Across the shoals, propelled by oars.
On holiday, some girl would sail to see
Her love and please a wealthy shepherd's heart.
And when her boat returned, the fertile land
Would send its gifts along as well,   60
Some cheese perhaps, or glistening,
The offspring of a snowy ewe.

"Aeneas, man of action -
And the brother too of Love,
That flits from place to place,   65
Aeneas, you who bear the gods
Of Troy upon your fleeing ships,
Now Jove himself assigns Laurentian fields
To you. The land bids welcome now,
Calls to your wandering household gods.   70
You'll be a hallowed presence there,
When waves they call Numician and bless
For years to come, consign you to the sky,
A native god yourself. And see,
How Victory flies above your weary ships;   75
At last she comes, at last,
Proud goddess, to your Trojan men.
And see: the fires burn for me

In the Rutilians' camp as well.
So Turnus, butcher, now I prophesy   80
Your death. Before my eyes, a Laurentian camp
Lies clear to see, walls of Lavinium
And Alba Longa too,
Which King Ascanius did build;
And Ilia now I see,   85
The priestess and delight of Mars,
Who left unwatched the Vestals' hearth.
I see them lying in embrace, Love's thieves,
Her headband tossed aside,
The armor of the god in love   90
Left lying on the river bank.
Now bulls, come crop the grass
Upon these seven hills, while time allows,
For here a mighty city soon shall rise.
Ah, Rome, your name is fated for the rule   95
Of all the lands where Ceres looks
From heaven on her fields,
Both where the sunrise spreads across the sky,
And where the streams of Ocean bathe
The panting horses of the sun.   100
Then Troy shall be astonished at herself,
Proclaim the care you took of her
On journeys long and far.
I tell what's true and truthful may I eat
The sacred laurel without harm,   105
Virginity be mine eternally."

All this the priestess spoke,
And called you, Phoebus, to herself,
Her tumbling hair all tossed across her face.
Whatever Amalthea sang,   110
Whatever in Marpessa Herophile spoke,
Advice which Grecian Phoeto gave,
And all the sacred lots
That Tibur's Sibyl carried dry,
Their words still clear, across the Anio's stream.   115
All said a comet would be seen,

An evil sign of war,
That many stones would rain upon the earth.
They told of horns, of rattling arms
Heard in the sky, of groves that prophesied   120
A rout, and then a murky year
Did see the sun itself deprived of light
While yoking horses that were pale,
And statues of the gods
That wept with luke-warm tears, and cows   125
With human voices telling fates to come.
These things all happened once.

But gentle now, Apollo, sink
These prodigies beneath
The unrelenting sea.   130
The kindled laurel burns with bright
And holy flames - an omen for the year to come,
Both bountiful and blessed;
For as the laurel grants good signs,
Farmers all, rejoice, since Ceres stacks   135
Your barns to bursting with her ears of corn.
Then stained with juice, the country folk
Will trample on the grapes
Until the jars and mammoth vats
Are brimmed to overflowing,   140
And, soaked with Bacchus' drink, the shepherd sings
To Pales, patron god, at festival:
"You wolves, keep far away from pens of ours."
Then, when they're drunk, they set the torch
To ritual stacks of dried-out hay   145
And leap across the holy flames.
Those days their wives give birth and children grasp
Their parents ears and kiss them loud.
Grandfather watches sleeping grandchild then
And never tires, talks baby-talk   150
When it awakes, despite his years.
In service to the god, the young
Lie on the grass, where darting shadows fall
From some old tree, or make a tent of clothes,

Stretched out and bound with ropes of flowers.   155
And flowers too will crown their cups,
As all make towers of the banquet fare,
With turf for tables, turf for couches too.
And then some boy who's drunk insults his girl
With words he'll later wish he could unsay   160
With the pledges that a lover gives.
For he who's cruel to one he loves
Will weep when sober, even he,
And swear his wits were gone. In this, your peace,
Away with bows, away with arrows too.   165
Please, Phoebus now, let Love unarmed
Sojourn on earth. A fine skill - Love's,
But after Cupid took his weapons up,
Alas, what grief his skill did bring,
And to what multitudes of men,   170
To me especially!

A year I've lain now with this wound,
Indulged disease. The pain itself
Gives me delight, while still I sing
My Nemesis, without whom words themselves,   175
The beat of all my verse would go astray.
A warning though for you:
The gods take care of poets, so...
Be gentle with this holy bard, and let me hymn
Our Messallinus when he drives   180
The prize of war: the towns he's sacked,
Before his car, the laurel on his brow;
And wild laurel on his men, who cry aloud:
"Io, Triumph," as they march along.
Then let my own Messalla give the crowd   185
The spectacle that piety requires,
And father, as the chariot rolls by,
Applaud his son.
Nod your approval, Phoebus, come;
And if you do, wear fair long hair   190
And hold your sister near you, chaste,
In perpetuity.

Commentary

In this, the longest and most ambitious poem of the collection Tibullus comes close to abandoning his elegiac voice for the voice of an epic poet, treating as he skirts the generic boundary a number of his favorite themes: war and peace, city and country, sex and violence and, above all, the relationship of time to the timeless and eternal. As we have already seen, these themes are presented in the form of a hymn to Apollo, which includes a poetic reverie in which the imagination of the poet wanders, to some degree free, to some degree constrained by the ritual which is taking place: by its sights, sounds and form. On this level the poem is, therefore, a mental reflection of the ritual and is bound into a ring by the image of the statue of Apollo which is addressed at both the opening and the close of the elegy.

Beneath the surface of this reverie, however, a second level of organization may be discerned. Examined more closely, the poem can be viewed as a meditation upon the changing and insubstantial world of human affairs, a world which the poet views as bound by both time and space. His treatment of time is especially ingenious. Using the present event, the young Messallinus' induction into the priesthood responsible for keeping and consulting the Sibylline books of prophecy, he is able to treat the remote and recent past, ancient Rome and the civil wars of his own centuries, as if they were future events, as events given in prophecy. Then, after returning to the present ritual, the poet examines both an immediate and a remoter future which the ritual's good omens promise: the prosperity to be enjoyed by farmers in the seasons to follow and the future achievements of Messallinus in his adult years. At the close of the elegy the poet reverses the time warp, briefly viewing the future as past, suggesting that Messallinus has already accomplished his military successes by describing the triumph that will follow and mark his deeds. The effect of all of these devices is to shatter time, to make it seem unreal, a mere illusion behind which greater truth lies concealed.

This is no less so in the case of space, whose reality grows weaker and weaker as the elegy unfolds. Troy becomes Rome, rural land becomes a great city, the city extends its rule back to Troy and even beyond it. And in the present, in the wake of the civil turmoil in the poet's own century, the promises of the ritual held in the city are fulfilled first in the country at a rural festival, then in distant lands with the victories of Messalinus and finally in the city again with his triumph. Thus space becomes little more than a fluid medium in which destiny is worked out through human endeavor.

What is eternally destined and constant is, of course, the central concern of the poem. It is this concern for the *destiny* of both the individual and the community that gives this elegy, which is in a sense a miniature *Aeneid*, its epic tone. This treatment of the unchanging and eternal takes two forms in the poem. First, the permanence and immortality of the divine is again and again contrasted with the changing and illusory nature of human events in time and space. The central symbol of this permanence is the statue of the god Apollo, whose hair itself, one of the least substantial parts of human beauty, remains ever the same and beautiful. Linked to Apollo are both the Sibyls and his sister Diana for all of whom their chastity is a symbol of their unchanging nature and reliability. For this reason, the opposition of chastity to sexuality is a recurring theme in the elegy, a theme which is developed in two parallel movements of three steps each. The first movement lies in the past and includes Ilia, a holy figure who has been violated, the girl who rows across the Velabrum, a human figure engaging in what appears to be idyllic sexuality, and the Sibyl, a divinely possessed priestess who remains ever chaste. The second movement is located in the present and future and includes rustic human lovers engaged in rather crude sexual banter, then the promiscuous Nemesis, the poet's own beloved, and finally Diana herself, the very symbol of purity and the eternally chaste divine.

The poet is not content, however, with a mere contrast of the changing and the permanent, the human and divine. He is interested as well in the intersection of the two. The intersection occurs, he suggests in this elegy, through revelation and prophecy, as exemplified by the Sibyls and by other seers and poets inspired by Apollo; and, of course, through the destined accomplishments of individual men: Aeneas, Romulus, Messalla and Messallinus. The symbol of these intersections is the laurel, a tree which grew in abundance on Mount Parnassus itself, seat of divine prophecy, and which provided a crown for priests and prophets, gods and heroes. The role of the laurel as a sign of the eternal present in human affairs is unmistakable here. As opposed to the grosser food of the picnicking farmers and shepherds, the Sibyl consumes the laurel and is inspired by it. When the laurel burns, it reveals good omens of what is predestined. Finally, the laurel wreath which appears on the head of Apollo at the beginning of the poem appears at its close on the brow of

Messallinus. The divine has penetrated the human in the realm of both idea and act. We can see, then, that the ring structure of the poem which begins and ends with the statue of the god, takes on deeper significance, for the divine sign, the laurel, is in fact transferred from the god to his human surrogate, the young hero.

A final question about this extraordinary elegy. Is it in fact elegiac or epic, and, if it is truly is an elegy, wherein lies its lament? In answering this question, one must first take into account the situation of Tibullus and of other poets who wrote under the Augustan regime for patrons who to one degree or another subscribed to that regime's ideological and political vision. Tibullus, like his contemporaries, was not entirely free. He was no doubt expected to produce in this elegy a text that would please his patron Messalla and not offend the sensibilities of the regime. What he produces in response is a text behind which this very problem lingers, a text in which the poetic voice employs complex Hellenistic techniques to manipulate the emotional and imagistic registers in such a way that subtle subtexts appear. If we read carefully we become aware of the striking of disconcerting minor chords throughout the elegy: the fact that the girl in her skiff brings back rich gifts, one of Tibullus' favorite negative symbols, the burning of Troy, the violation of Ilia, the omens of the civil war, the behavior of the rustic lover and the poet's treatment at the hands of Nemesis. The striking of these notes is not only symptomatic of Tibullus' dilemma, it is also an invitation to read the elegy as an *elegy*, not as Messalla or Augustus would read it, but against the grain. In short, this elegy, like the *Aeneid*, invites its own deconstruction by the reader. Perhaps the penetration of the human by the divine is not as certain and sublime as we would wish. The darkness of the elegiac world still lies in the shadows just beyond Apollo's temple and the firelight of a rustic festival.

✦   ✦   ✦

2.6

Introduction

The poet is reflecting sardonically upon the fact that a friend named Macer, very possibly the fellow poet Pompeius Macer, has decided to go off on a military expedition, either literally or poetically or both, the very enterprise, we recall, that was so emphatically eschewed in the very first elegy of the collection. He calls upon Cupid himself to call Macer back to his true vocation, love, and then adds that if in fact Cupid is easy on lovers who go off to war, he too will join the army and go along with his friend.

The boast is hollow, he confesses at once, admitting that he himself is utterly incapable of deserting his mistress and that Love is in fact not easy on lovers but a cruel torturer of them. So painful is his suffering, he admits, that he is driven to blaspheming the god and contemplating suicide itself. It is in fact only Hope that keeps him from taking his own life, for Hope keeps telling him that his Nemesis will soon be his, deluding him just as she deludes men in chains with a false vision of freedom.

In his desperation the poet then employs a new and bizarre strategy. It seems that his mistress' little sister has recently been killed in a tragic plunge from an upstairs window. It is to this child that the poet now directs Nemesis' attention. He will, he tells her, attend the child's grave and she in turn, taking pity on him, will, should Nemesis not relent, return in her bloodied state to haunt her cruel sister. Even this project is, however, beyond his powers; he cannot bear the thought of his Nemesis in tears. And so, he turns instead to her procuress, to Phryne, whose name in Greek means "toad," and accuses her of both having

corrupted her naturally good mistress and having thwarted his love.
How has she done this? With words, by carrying secret messages to
rival lovers and by lying to the poet by telling him that his mistress is
absent even when he can hear Nemesis' voice within the house. The
elegy and the collection can only be brought to a conclusion by the
words of a curse on this old woman, the evil genius of his love, a curse
so grim and complete that even its partial fulfillment will leave the
woman in pain.

Translation

Macer is enlisting;
Now what about tender Love?
Will he go too, as his side-kick,
Like some hero hanging weapons
Around his neck, make long marches   5
With a mortal, sail upon the vagrant sea,
Be willing with his blade drawn
To stand beside his pal?
Sweet Cupid, I beseech you,
Brand that arrogant legionnaire,   10
Who has left your life of ease,
A deserter! Bring him back again
To the camp that you command.

But if, in fact, you're easy on recruits,
Here's another trooper   15
Who will carry slopping water
In his helmet as a jug, join
The army, leaving Venus and the girls.
I'm as tough as any man is;
They can sound the charge for me.   20
Just boasting, boasting that,
And when, a loud-mouthed fool, I boast,
Slammed doors cut short bravado's litany.
How many times I've sworn
Never again to knock upon that door   25
And then, when I had duly sworn,
My foot turned back once more!

But, bitter Love, I wish,
If it is proper, that I could see
Your arrows snapped in two, your torches quenched,   30
For in my wound of woe you twist
The knife and make me pray for things
That foreshadow my own doom,
And with a mind that's mad say things
That never should be said by men.   35
And now I'd make an end of woe in death,
But Hope that makes us trusting coaxes,
Fondles life and always says
Tomorrow will be better than today.
Hope nourishes the farmer, Hope   40
Believes the seed sown now
Within the furrowed land will bring
A tidy profit from the fields.
It's Hope that snares the birds in nets,
The fish on lines, when tiny hooks   45
Hang hidden behind bait. It's Hope
That comforts the strong-shackled slave;
His ankles make an iron sound,
But as he works, he sings. It's Hope
That promised me that Nemesis   50
Would come to bed, but she refused.

Unbending woman, ah, don't make
A goddess kneel. Give in, I beg,
By your own sister's bones that lie
All out of season in the grave;   55
Then let the child sleep in peace
Beneath the gentle earth.
For she is holy still to me,
And I shall place my gifts upon her grave,
A garland moist with tears of mine;   60
Flee to her mound, sit suppliant, lament
My fate to ashes that cannot reply.
The child will not forever bear
A faithful mourner's tears provoked by you.
And so, at her command, I say   65

You must not be so grudging with your love.

Then ghosts who've been ignored
Will send no evil dreams;
Your grieving sister will not stand
Before your bed while you're asleep -   70
The way she looked, when from the upper floor
Headlong she fell and bloodied came
To the lakes that lie below.
But stop. I will not stir again
My mistress' bitter grief.   75
I am not worth a single moment's sob.
Nor does she deserve to have
Those eyes that speak made red with tears.
That woman who procures her men,
She does the harm. The girl herself is good.   80
That bawd, that Phryne stabs my grieving heart.
She comes and goes, all on the sly,
And carries letters hidden in her gown;
And often, at their unrelenting door,
When I've heard my mistress' honied voice,   85
She says she's not at home;
And often, when the night is mine
By promises she gave,
The woman says the girl is tired
And languishing. She claims she fears   90
Some threats that have been made, and then
I die with longing and anxiety.
My mind, unravelling,
Imagines who her lover is
And all the ways the two make love.   95
Then, Phryne, I call down a curse on you.
You'll taste your fill, your fill
Of painful worry in this life,
If but the smallest portion of my prayer
Can move divinity.   100

Commentary

Some readers have been disappointed by this elegy both because of its own structure and content and because of its position in the collection. Is it complete or perhaps unfinished? And beyond that, does it provide a fitting capstone to the two books of poems? These are questions worthy of our concern as we complete our reading of Tibullus.

On the simplest level, the level of dramatic and psychological plausibility, the reply must be, I believe, in the affirmative. The love-sick poet's discourse is, as it has been in earlier elegies, credible and the elegiac moment described does not lack verisimilitude. The poet contemplates abandoning love with his friend Macer but realizes at once that his passion will not allow him to do it. He recalls his suffering at Love's hands, admits contemplating suicide and then reflects on the nature of Hope, which is what keeps him alive. Begging his mistress to relent, he calls up the memory of her dead sister and suggests that the sister may haunt her if she remains stubborn. Then, still mastered by his love, he withdraws this threat and blames instead the girl's procuress whom he curses as the poem draws to a close. There is nothing in this that is unclear, psychologically implausible or artistically incoherent.

The elegy is even more tightly structured on the thematic level. Four themes are interwoven in its text: desire, hope, violence and betrayal. Indeed the elegy is a study of their relationship to one another. This study is presented in five imagistic panels: the vision of the military life, the torture of the poet by Love, the meditation upon Hope, the appeal to Nemesis through her dead sister and the curse on Phryne, the procuress. In each of these panels there is one especially striking image: the soldier balancing water in a helmet, the broken arrows and extinguished torches of Love, the slave singing in his chains, the little girl plunging from the window and the procuress carrying secret messages in her gown. These images act as focal points in the poem and its effect on the reader is produced to a large degree by the tensions and resonances set up between them.

The elegy begins with the betrayal of Love, who is pictured as a tender god. The betrayal is accomplished through escape. Macer is turning his back on pleasure and romance by becoming a soldier, an act which will require strong purpose and delicate balance, as the helmet image suggests. In the following panel we discover that the poet is in fact incapable of this kind of concentration and restraint. For him Love is not tender; he is a cruel and violent torturer, whose instruments the poet wants to see broken and extinguished, who in fact drives the poet to the brink of suicide.

Why then does he go on? Because of Hope, he explains, picturing Hope not as a positive force in human affairs but as a cruel deceiver of mankind. Hope deceives both individuals and Love itself by holding out objects of desire that can never be attained. In its clutches the lover is like the slave who sings in chains, deluded by the hope that neither death nor escape need concern him, that a better day will come of its own accord. The fourth panel presents a vivid example of Hope dashed, here through violent death. The little girl, an image of desire yet to be and a poetic surrogate for both Love and Nemesis, is violently destroyed, plunging from her window to the underworld and then reappearing as the bloody ghost of vanished beauty. In this vision the present panel demonstrates that all of the earlier images, the balanced water in the helmet, the arrows of Love, a slave's hope, are all betrayers. The dreams of both escape and fulfillment are illusions which bring violent destruction and the haunting presence of what is in fact forever lost.

The poet returns as the poem closes to his own painful betrayal by Phryne. She carries no water in a helmet. Rather what she carefully balances in the folds of her gown are the secret letters, the instruments by which Love, Hope and the poet are all betrayed. Phryne betrays through her falsehood and thus removes from the poet the object of his longing and his hope, just as her little sister was violently removed from life.

What then of the elegy's position in the collection? Does it provide a fitting close? In responding to this question, we should first of all note the thematic resonances with other poems in the collection. Note for instance that this poem begins by drawing the same contrast between military endeavor and amatory endeavor that was drawn at the beginning of the very first elegy. And beyond that, many other references to themes treated in the first book recur: the torture of the lover, his delusion, the obsession with rival lovers and with the older woman who acts as the mistress' protectress and agent. The resonance with earlier themes in the second book are, perhaps, even more striking and significant. In this regard the juxtaposition of Hope and Nemesis is, it seems to me, of special importance. Taken as abstract concepts these two words suggest exact opposites. Hope promises a bright future in which one's dreams and illusions come true. Nemesis, on the other hand, promises vengeance and vindication, the price that must be paid for illusionary folly. The confrontation of these two future-focused forces in this elegy is not, I think fortuitous. Their presence here underlines what we found above: that whether she is Delia under another name or another girl, Nemesis is, above all, the poet's moment of reckoning, the instrument through whom he learns the bitter and elegiac truth that his hopes for amatory bliss are, in fact, in vain.

One further note. This elegy acts, it strikes me, as a capstone in another way, in that it acts as a kind of linguistic footnote to the rest of the collection. Examined from yet another perspective, its text is a commentary on the nature of language, its powers, positive and negative, and its weaknesses. The poem begins with the poet's boasts, which are quickly branded as false. In the next panel, the poet goes on to report that he has spoken things that men should never speak and then focuses on the false promises of Hope and the foolish singing of the chained slave. The panel that deals with dead girl is, seen from this perspective, a study of the limited powers of language and the greater powers of visual imagery, for the girl who cannot speak to the poet at the grave, is able with her mere appearance to communicate powerfully with the living. Finally, in treating the role of the procuress Phryne, Tibullus presents a complex matrix of images that convey the use and misuse of language. The poet hears his mistress' true voice even as Phryne lies to him about her absence. The spoken word is then transformed into the written words which Phryne carries in her gown, true in that they reflect Nemesis' real desire, false in that they are hidden from the poet and others. In this faulty and slippery linguistic realm, what can the poet do with language as his elegy and the collection to which it belongs draws to a close? He will use language to form a curse. Even here, in his very last lines, however, the efficacy of the curse's language is said to be in all likelihood only partial, and its power is seen as wholly dependent on the gods. What is Tibullus saying about the powers of a poetic text here? What ironic warning is he giving his reader?

✦   ✦   ✦

Afterword

The translations and comments in this book have attempted to demonstrate that Tibullus was an extraordinary poet with powerful and original insights into the human condition, and with an impressive range of poetic skills with which to express them. It might be appropriate here to look back at and summarize what we have found.

First, as I believe most critics would agree, Tibullus is a poet whose subtle poetic techniques must be carefully studied and understood if he is to be fully appreciated. It is, for example, necessary to understand, as one begins to read, the manner in which he manipulates and employs the poetic or elegiac voice. We have seen again and again that this voice, the voice I have referred to as "the poet," almost always speaks from a state of altered consciousness. This is not to say that the poet suffers from serious mental illness or from some cognitive dysfunction. It is to say that his thought is nearly always affected by some circumstance either inside his mind or in the poetic world he inhabits and that this circumstance is destabilizing to some degree. Sometimes it is fear or passion. sometimes illness or drunkenness, sometimes the demands of the moment in which he finds himself, a formal celebration, a ritual or a party. Whatever it is, it frees the poet from the constraints of everyday diction and rhetorical logic and enables him, without loss of verisimilitude, to think poetically and to move in his text both through time and space and through a complex metaphorical grid which plays upon both erudite and fanciful associations and harmonies.

We should not be surprised therefore to find that the true structure of the individual elegies, although they often parody or imitate more formal genres and forms, often lies beneath the surface, at a level at which resonating images and syntactical markers play a more decisive role than is at first obvious. What seems randomly or even ill-organized at the surface turns out again and again to be organized with great poetic subtlety, and it is often the case that the surface message of the text is not in fact its only or even primary message. Beneath the poet's facade of altered consciousness lies the highly skillful arrangement of words, sounds and images that reveal the deeper insights that Tibullus himself is trying to give us.

It is not always easy to find the message beneath the poet's mask. Indeed, we have seen that another technique of Tibullus makes it especially difficult to do so. Tibullus is particularly fond of playing with his reader and turning his text into a verbal game. As many critics have pointed out, poems that start in one sub-genre finish in another. Elegies which seem at first to treat one topic in fact treat another, and again and again Tibullus withholds information from his reader, leaving him in suspense about what is going on in his text. It is not easy, therefore, to be a reader of these elegies. We are always having to be on our guard, like the reader of a detective story, for subtle signals that point toward a textual surprise that will be puzzling to the careless reader.

Perhaps the most neglected aspect of Tibullus' work is a proper consideration of his own unique elegiac vision. Much of the excellent criticism that has appeared in the latter part of the twentieth century has focused on his place in the literary tradition of ancient lyric poetry, upon language and upon historical and antiquarian questions. This work is, of course, of enormous value and importance. It has tended, however, with some exceptions, to give too little attention to Tibullus, the original poet, who uses the tradition and its forms, to express something quite different and new. This elegiac vision, as I have called it, is the second aspect of the poetry that I hope the translations and discussions above have brought into clearer focus.

What I have suggested is that Tibullus, in all of the elegies, was aiming at conveying a single and coherent view of life, one which suggests over and over again that the realm of human action is an unstable realm, in which we must struggle, love and, oftener than not, suffer. It is a realm which always falls short of our vision of the idealized world of divine beauty and goodness, one in which things are almost never what they seem or what we wish them to be. And more than that, Tibullus' world is infected by an equally destabilizing psychological uncertainty, that produces in different beholders wholly different visions of reality, that also produces in a single beholder different visions at different moments. For these two reasons, Tibullus' world is a profoundly sad one, instinct with disappointment at every level. This, it seems to me, is the deepest and grimmest message that Tibullus strove to communicate. It permeates his text and is present as a minor chord struck even in the lightest moments, in the quiet contemplation of contentment and in the enjoyment of innocent revelry and celebration. It is, of course, the very essence of the elegiac.

Two false suppositions about the understanding of Tibullus' poetry I hope I have helped to challenge, the autobiographical and the narrative fallacies. In recent years critics have given less attention to the question of whether the poems are guides to understanding the historical Tibullus and his life, and this is, I believe, a good thing. There are certainly some historical figures in the elegies, the great Messalla, his patron, among them, and several historical events are referred to, but it is clearly a mistake to read these poems as either history or autobiography. As I have noted above, the figures and events are translated by the poet into elements in his elegiac text, and there is little reason to believe that they were ever intended to inform us with any accuracy about the life of the writer and his acquaintances. Messalla may be, to some small degree, an exception here because of his stature and his role as patron, but even in his case it seems to me that the practice of writing history from elegy is an extremely dangerous one.

But there is a deeper problem. A good deal of recent criticism makes the equally questionable assumption that the elegies must form, when taken together, a coherent narrative, if not autobiographical then at least fictional. It is from this assumption that spring lengthy discussion about the identities of Delia and Nemesis, about the rich lovers and their relationships to the women and to Marathus, the homosexual beloved. It strikes me that there is little in Tibullus' text itself that supports this assumption. Figures reappear in several elegies, it is true, just as the same figure might appear in several paintings by the same painter, but this does not imply that a coherent narrative with a carefully worked out sequence of cause and effect is intended. As the discussions above indicate, I would argue that the figures in the elegies should be read not as figures in a novel or narrative poem, but as types that are used as correlatives to give substance to the poet's emotional dilemma at one moment or another. Delia and Nemesis are, in all likelihood the distillation of a dozen love affairs, and their behavior in the individual elegies should not be read as evidence of the course of a single love affair, but rather as symbols of the author's emotional journey through the harsh landscape of amatory delight and suffering. The line of movement in this text is not the line of narrative, it is a cognitive and emotional line that uses the resonance that recurring figures provide to illustrate states of mind and new intuitions about the human condition, about the suffering and grief that plague our lives. Delia and Nemesis, the rich husband/lover are not people in a story; they are types, artfully manipulated poetic stereotypes, that give flesh to the poet's vision and lament. In short, I would argue that we are meant to experience the elegies not as a modern novel or film but as a series of pictures in a gallery. Resonances, cross references, anaphors there may be, but not a plot and not a set of unchanging characters.

Because of all of these views, some generally accepted, some more provocative, I have suggested above some readings of the individual elegies that will be questioned by other critics, hopefully by students using this text as well. Some of these readings are deliberately unorthodox and intended to stimulate discussion. This is, after all, what a good textbook should do. Beneath the disagreement that bold readings produce, move the murky waters in which questions about the nature of criticism and the text itself lie in wait. As I glance in their direction, I will note only that our playful poet, who seemed to enjoy, even demand, an active reader, might have been delighted, even in his somewhat strait-laced literary world, to discover that his poems are interpreted in different ways. Therein lies, perhaps, his greatness.

✦   ✦   ✦

Select Bibliography

What follows is by no means a complete bibliography of works about Tibullus and his poetry. For one thing, given the likely readership of this book, the list has been limited to works written in English. Readers are alerted to the fact that most of the works cited require some knowledge of Latin, if they are to be read carefully. This should not, however, put Latinless readers off. A reader who is willing to consult a Latin dictionary from time to time should be able to follow the thoughts presented in these texts; and even the reader unwilling to make that effort will find much that is useful and enlightening in them. Readers who wish to pursue their critical reading further are directed to Harrauer's *Bibliography to the Corpus Tibullianum* and to Murgatroyd's *Tibullus, Elegies II,* both of which are cited below and provide much fuller bibliographical guidance.

Ball, R.J. *Tibullus the Elegist* (Gottingen, 1983).

Bright, D.F. *Haec Mihi Fingebam* (Leiden, 1978).

Cairns, F. *Tibullus: A Hellenistic Poet at Rome* (Cambridge, 1979).

Copley, F.O. *Exclusus Amator: A Study in Latin Love Poetry* (Madison, 1956).

Harraurer,H. *A Bibliography to the Corpus Tibullianum* (Hildesheim, 1971).

Harrington, K.P. *The Roman Elegiac Poets* (Norman, 1968).

Lee, A.G. and Maltby, R. *Tibullus: Elegies* (Liverpool, 1990).

Luck, G. *Latin Love Elegy* (London, 1969).

Lyne, R.O.A.M. *The Latin Love Poets from Catullus to Horace* (Oxford, 1980).

Maltby, R. *Latin Love Elegy* (Bristol, 1980).

Murgatroyd, P. *Tibullus I* (Pietermaritzburg, 1980; reprinted Bristol, 1991).

------- *Tibullus, Elegies II* (Oxford, 1994).

Platnauer, M. *Latin Elegiac Verse* (Cambridge, 1951).

Putnam, M.C.J. *Tibullus: A Commentary* (Norman, 1973).

✦✦✦

BIOGRAPHY: GEORGE W. SHEA

George W. Shea was born in 1934 in Paterson, N.J. He received his B.A. from Fordham University and his M.A. and PhD in Classics from Columbia University. He returned to Fordham to teach Classics in 1967 and in 1970 was appointed Dean of Fordham College at Lincoln Center, a post which he held for fifteen years. He returned to the classroom in 1985 and has been teaching Classics and Comparative Literature at the College since then. He is the author of many articles and reviews on both classical and general topics and of The Poems of Alcimus Ecdicius Avitus, published by Medieval and Renaissance Texts and Studies in 1997.

Dr. Shea is married to Shirley Ashton, who holds a B.A. and M.A. in modern languages from Oxford University and who was for many years a member of the language faculty at Fairleigh Dickinson University. The Sheas have three children: Sarah, Susan and George Michael.

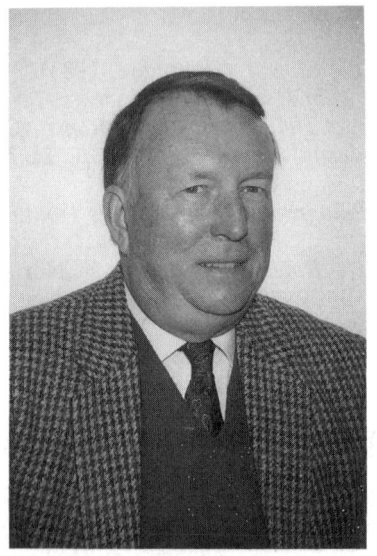